CHARACTERS OF CRICKET

CHARACTERS OF CRICKET

DAN WHITING
FROM THE MIDDLE STUMP

Front cover images © PA Images.

First published 2015

The History Press
The Mill, Brimscombe Port
Stroud, Gloucestershire, GL5 2QG
www.thehistorypress.co.uk

British Library Cataloguing in Publication Data.
A catalogue record for this book is available from the British Library.

ISBN 978 0 7509 6112 7

Typesetting and origination by The History Press
Printed in Great Britain

I am really pleased to be writing a few more words for the author of *Cricket Banter* and *Characters of Cricket*. The second title is very appropriate as there are some lovely characters in the world of cricket, a lot of whom have been very kind to Melanoma UK in the last few years.

If the second book is half as good as the first, I am looking forward to plenty of anecdotal evidence that will make me smile.

We are grateful to Dan and The Middle Stump team for the continued support of Melanoma UK. Melanoma continues to be a very serious issue in the UK, and through the game of cricket, we have been able to educate many people on the need for a careful approach during hot and sunny weather.

Gill Nuttall, 2015
Melanoma UK

FOREWORD

One of the most likeable and beguiling aspects of cricket is its characters. C.L.R. James wrote:

What do they know of cricket who only cricket know?

The cast of cricketers here don't fall foul of James' concern, as becomes clear pretty quickly. Here we read numerous stories that demonstrate the versatility and breadth of many cricketers' interests and experiences.

It's often said that this game is a metaphor for life, and this is reflected many times in the tales of the people who've woven the tapestry of the game so many of us love. This book also examines the work of art that is the contemporary product in England and Wales. The recollections of the men and women who adorn our national summer game are rich with humour and camaraderie. Many accounts stir the soul; I found the 'Prince of Wales' (Matt Maynard) account did just that for me. In playing with my feelings it did four things: I chuckled, it made me relive an experience, forced me to Google and to reread a eulogy, and the emotions it stirred stung my eyes. It did exactly what a good book should.

Cricket, as we followers know only too well, regularly confounds its fans and pundits. Consider this typical prose from one of Yorkshire's finest:

> The Aussies have spent so much time basking in the glory of the last generation that they have forgotten to plan for this one. It's just like the West Indies again; once their great names from the 1970s and 80s retired, the whole thing fell apart. The way things are going, the next Ashes series cannot come too quickly for England. What a shame that we have to wait until 2013 to play this lot again.
>
> *Geoffrey Boycott*

If you take yourself too seriously, the game has the knack of returning you to earth, and often none too elegantly.

However, I am sure that Geoffrey is now aware that since his quote, the Australian team well and truly returned the English lads to earth, and with a bang!

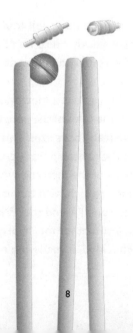

The author, Dan Whiting, is a passionate cricket fan and finds time to chair the redoubtable Southgate Adelaide Cricket Club in Greater London, as well as trying to meet his grocery bills and match fees as a recruitment specialist in the legal profession. Dan has set out to provide a fresh and rather irreverent angle on cricket and the numbers of followers of his site, The Middle Stump, and its social media offspring, are testimony to the niche it's managed to carve out. It's also of note that followers and contributors include many past and present cricketers and other notable sportsmen from near and far. These include Graeme Fowler, Matt Maynard, Jason Gillespie, Alan Mullally, Mike Gatting, Paul Nixon and many more who have all contributed to the laughs and jokes included on his web page.

This compendium of characters is a fine addition to the game's history. It will bring considerable pleasure, and enhance the knowledge of all those who choose to dip into it.

I hope that you enjoy it as much as I do.

Andy Nash, Chairman of Somerset County Cricket Club
2015

ACKNOWLEDGEMENTS

I would like to thank the following for their help in the making of *Characters of Cricket*:

My kids, who are my *raison d'être* – Rebecca, Hannah, Ben and Beth. To John Thorp, for his article on 'oppo speak' and being an all-round good bloke for the last thirty years; Andy Nash, the Chairman of Somerset County Cricket Club, who so kindly wrote the foreword for this book; to Liam Kenna, my old partner in crime at The Middle Stump; John Cosgrove, Reckless, Pinstripe Pete, Jamie Parker, Jeff Searle, Paul Ruffhead and Neil Manvell and all the boys in Barnet; to the boys and girls of Southgate Adelaide CC in north London (if Carlsberg did cricket clubs …); Danish, Eros, Sparrow, Worthy, Greg Mackett and many more; Anthony Morris and Adam Whiting; Brian 'Oz' Cohen; John Simpson and Gareth Berg at Middlesex CCC; to Graeme 'Foxy' Fowler; Matt Maynard for his kind words; the Shantry brothers – Adam and Jack – for their wonderful stories; the legend Steve Kirby at Somerset CCC; the 'Headband Warrior' at Yorkshire CCC, Jack Brooks;

Ryan Sidebottom, a splendid ambassador for Melanoma UK; Steve Gale and Scott Ruskin at Hertford; Paul Nixon for his general bonhomie; Amy; George Berry, Gena and Ruth; Richard Whiting in Cardiff; Fred Boycott; Paul Mokler; Susan Usher; Nik Myles in Nottinghamshire, and all who have helped us via Twitter; George Dobell for his words of encouragement when starting out; Nigel Walker, Nigel Henderson and the chaps at *Guerilla Cricket*; John Etheridge of the *Sun*; all at The History Press; Steve James and Hugh Bateson at the *Telegraph* for correcting my spelling, grammar and entering into debates with us; Marcus Charman and the Cricket Family; Langwith CC; anyone and everyone who has helped promote us and for their support over the years; and all those who have bought a copy of this book.

Finally to my mum, who gave me the support and encouragement to play this wonderful game when I was a kid: without that, I wouldn't have written this book.

Gill Nuttall at Melanoma UK and all those suffering from this cruel disease – this one goes out to you.

> I tend to think that cricket is the greatest thing that God ever created on earth – certainly greater than sex, although sex isn't too bad either.
>
> *Harold Pinter*

character

[kar–ik–ter]

---

noun

1   the aggregate of features and traits that form the individual nature of some person or thing.
2   one such feature or trait; characteristic.
3   moral or ethical quality: a man of fine, honourable character.
4   qualities of honesty, courage, or the like; integrity.
5   reputation: a stain on one's character.

INTRODUCTION

Cricket is a game that attracts many characters. From the village green to the professional game – whether it is that maverick amateur from your fourth eleven who always has too much to drink on a Saturday night in the clubhouse, or the bloke who the tabloid press won't leave alone – there are many throughout this wonderful sport.

It is why I wanted to write this book. For me, cricket is about these people and as much about having a few beers at the end of play as it is watching it on your television. Everyone who has made it into this book has enhanced the game and has put bums on seats: whether they are the good guys, the bad guys or even the ugly, they are the reason why people pay good money to go and watch the sport. Yes, of course there is something of great beauty about a David Gower cover drive, but to me, cricket is so much more than just what is played out on the pitch, and to watch the guys you will shortly read about joke, laugh, snarl, or in other cases, get up to far worse, is why we love cricket.

Many I have grown up with, during an era where the game was less professional and the foibles of your average sportsman were laid bare for the public to see. The idiosyncratic ways of players of yesteryear often make far better material than today's media savvy, monotone interviewees, but still the odd person from the modern era takes their place in the book.

Many of the stories in this book and my first, *Cricket Banter*, have been part of my childhood in Hertfordshire and north London club cricket. The days of sides playing it hard but fair on the pitch and having four or five pints together are dying out, and many local club cricketing characters, in turn, are also departing the grass roots scene. I look to write about these anecdotes, and the characters that have influenced my formative years and enhanced my love for the game.

So, what actually defines character? Character is about showing honourable qualities, courage, integrity or moral fibre, or standing out from the crowd. I would suggest that everyone in this book has those qualities. Anyone who has faced a quick bowler or played sport at a decent level will understand what I am talking about. As Theodore Roosevelt famously once said:

> The credit belongs to the man who is actually in the arena, whose face is marred by dust and sweat and blood; who strives valiantly; who errs, who comes short again and again, because there is no effort without error and shortcoming; but who does actually strive to do the deeds; who knows great enthusiasms, the great devotions; who spends himself in a worthy cause; who at the best knows in the end the triumph of high achievement, and who at the worst, if he fails, at least fails while daring greatly, so that his place shall never be with those cold and timid souls who neither know victory nor defeat.

Saying that, hats off to the No. 11 who has potted it out for a draw too! Many of those who regularly bat at this number make it into this book, funnily enough. However, the quality that all of the people you are about to read about have is the ability to distinguish themselves from others who have played the game. They are people you remember, the ones that stick out from your childhood, the ones who made you laugh, the ones who you feel a sense of affinity with, and the ones you want to see do well, sometimes even though they are playing for the opposition. To use a modern and vulgar term, they have the 'X factor'.

From Shane Warne and Ian Botham to Leslie Hylton, the only cricketer to be hanged; or the obscure county professionals from the early 1980s: the mad, like Derek Randall; the bad, such as the match fixers; or the downright ugly (too numerous to name!), these are the people who define the game for me, and are an integral part of why I love this wonderful sport. Whether it is the grace of Gower, the joviality of Phil Tufnell, the sledging of Shane Warne, or Mark Vermeulen with a box of Swan Vestas in his hand, these people were all individuals and stood out from the crowd.

And for that, I adore them.

Dan Whiting
April 2014

I feel when somebody has
been playing cricket for
a long time, he creates a
separate identity for himself.

S.R. Tendulkar

MY HERO

David Ivon Gower was my hero. Whilst not being one of the major characters of the game, he was the man who did it for me as a kid. (I had posters up on my wall.) This is *my* book so he is going to come first – so there.

I loved Gower, to the extent that I even had a cat called Gower. I first noticed him, David that is and not my cat, during a John Player League game in 1977, one that was affected by rain. All of a sudden BBC2 went from showing the cricket to classical music with a pair of wicketkeeping gloves, and this bored kid had nothing to do. Classical music also is what they would play on Radio 3, back in the day, when the cricket was washed out, and I have had an inbuilt hatred of that bastard Beethoven ever since.

Gower came to prominence in 1978, when England were decimated due to Packer call-ups. The likes of Clive Radley and David were picked to play against Pakistan and, having received a short ball from the trundling Liaqat Ali, he pulled it for 4. Not a bad way to play your first ball in Test cricket now is it? He finished with 58, and had a good season, culminating in a splendid hundred against the New Zealanders later in the summer at the Oval.

Gower was amazing to watch. As someone said, 'He made it look so easy until he made a mistake. Sometimes the mistake was put off for long enough for him to play an innings of individual brilliance'. His cover drives were a thing of beauty – the lazy flick off his legs, the swivel pull – the whole thing was majestic, almost effortless, and he still remains for me, the most beautiful batsman of all time.

Azharuddin, Mark Waugh, Stephen Fleming all come close, but Gower was my god. Yes, he would nick off to the slips, yes, he would do something stupid, yes, he would throw it away, but in this child's eyes, he was the main man. Almost to the point where you would be willing Brearley to get out, just so you could watch him bat. I even wished I was left-handed at times.

Gower then had a sparkling 1979, apt for a man who enjoyed the odd glass of champers. A hundred against the Aussies in Perth, facing a fired-up Rodney Hogg was followed up in England by a double hundred against India.

Unfortunately, 1980 was a tough year, and he was dropped having been worked over by the touring West Indians. Despite being picked to tour the Windies, and scoring a magical 154 at Sabina Park in a tour marred by the death of Kenny Barrington, he didn't score many in the 1981 Home Series against Australia, and was eventually dropped for Paul Parker for the final Test.

It was during this time that Gower was even parodied for the classic TV series *Not the Nine O'Clock News*, when he dropped an infamous skier during a game. The sketch showed Griff Rhys Jones pushing very hard to defecate in an aeroplane toilet before releasing his stool of gargantuan proportions, then the clip shifted to David dropping the aforementioned 'bum Havana'.

The 1982 series saw Gower perform well, and in 1983 he scored an amazing hundred in the World Cup. He also took over the England captaincy, firstly as understudy to the injured Bob Willis, before getting the gig in 1984. Unfortunately it was against the West Indies, and England were 'blackwashed', losing the series 5–0. Gower even set them 300 once, in less than a day at Lord's, but Gordon Greenidge saw to that with the most unbelievable double hundred in two sessions.

He managed to keep the captaincy for the tour of India, and led the side extremely well during what can only be described as the most difficult tour ever. The assassination of Mrs Gandhi led to rioting and mass murder across the country. They even went to a party at British High Commissioner Percy Norris' house, only to wake up and find that he had been murdered the following day. Despite this, they continued and Gower became only the second Englishman after Douglas Jardine to win in India.

The 1985 season can only be described as Gower's 'glorious summer'. Skippering a side to beat the Aussies is what every English schoolboy dreams of, and his hundred in the Texaco Series, before the Tests kicked off, was merely the hors d'oeuvres before he tucked into the main course. His 166 at Trent Bridge was my favourite ever Gower knock and has been watched countless times on YouTube. Madonna may have been No. 1 with 'Into the Groove' that summer but Gower was seriously in the groove with a double hundred at Edgbaston, his 215 being his highest Test score, before the *coup de grâce* of 157 at the Oval. To watch Gooch smashing it with his cudgel, and Gower delightfully wafting his wand, caressing it around south London, was to watch the antithesis of batting as they put on 300.

It was after this that it started to go a bit wrong for Gower, although he did lead his side to domestic success in the Benson & Hedges Trophy. Another 'blackwash' in the West Indies, and the knives were out amongst the press pack. Mike Gatting soon got the job and, Gower being Gower, famously passed him a t-shirt with 'I'm in charge' written on it.

The summer of 1988 was infamous for being the summer of four England captains, including Chris Cowdrey, and English cricket was a complete shambles. Gower continued to churn out the runs, and in 1989 he was reinstated as England captain for the visit of the Aussies, despite the TCCB having promised Gatt the job. Again the press got on his back, so at one point during a press conference he announced that he had tickets to the theatre and promptly walked out. Can you imagine an England captain doing that now? It was another horrific summer, blighted by stories of rebel tours to South Africa and a good Australian team. He lost his job at the end of that year, and it was the beginning of the end for him.

Graham Gooch took over, and his fitness regime never really fitted in with David's ethos. The famous 'Tiger Moth' incident, where he hired a plane from a local airfield before dive-bombing

his mate Robin Smith, went down really badly, but not as badly with Gooch as getting out a couple of balls before lunch flicking down the leg side, caught at long leg. When Gower was good, he was marvellous. When he was bad, he was really bad.

Despite getting runs against Waqar and Wasim in 1992, a series blighted by ball-tampering rows, Gower was dropped and, despite some MCC members calling for an emergency General Meeting trying to reinstate him, that was that. Sadly, my cat Gower died shortly afterwards too, and went to the grave with a bit of my childhood. His life mirrored Gower's Test career, lithesome as a youngster but becoming frail and elderly-looking towards the end. He even started to lose his fur!

Achieving 117 Tests and 8,231 Test runs, with 3,000 in One Day cricket, meant Gower was a legend of English cricket. His fielding was brilliant at times, whether in the covers as a young man before a shoulder injury curtailed his athleticism, and his bravery close to the bat, especially to Edmonds or Emburey, should also not be forgotten. His off-spin, however, can be consigned to the dustbin, although he did manage one Test wicket. He was famous for his declaration bowling in a game for Leicestershire, in which Steve O'Shaughnessy hit the fastest hundred. Gower's figures were 9–0–102–0!

He finished his career at Hampshire, and he is now the anchor of Sky Sports cricket coverage. I will remember him for his panache, his grace and his wonderful cover drives. Gower was truly my hero as a child, and for that he is first in my book.

A STAR IS WARNE

Shane Keith Warne was born on 13 September 1969 in Melbourne, and revolutionised the game of cricket. Leg spinners were a dying breed up until the 1990s when he exploded on to the scene, and he was certainly the finest bowler that I have ever witnessed. The previous twenty or so years before his arrival within the Test arena were all about pace, with the West Indian battery of quicks, followed by the toe-crushing pace of Waqar Younis and Wasim Akram. Shane Warne changed all that. The beach-blonde young Australian had arrived on the scene, looking as if he had arrived straight off a surfboard, or the cast of *Home and Away*, and kids went from trying to bowl quickly to flipping it out of the back of their wrist.

Leg spinners were supposed to be dying out, the modern day pitches not conducive to their art, and I had only seen a few in my time. The Australians, Richie Benaud and Terry Jenner, were before my time and Bob Holland was barely good enough, save one performance against England at Lord's. Abdul Qadir was probably the best that I had seen, although I had listened to the radio as Laxman Sivaramakrishnan span us out in India in 1984. All of the above could be brilliant on their day, but leg spinners were deemed a luxury due to being expensive, and One Day cricket had killed them off. Again, Shane Warne changed that.

A budding Aussie rules footballer, he was let go before arriving in Bristol to play club cricket in 1989. It was here that he first came to light in England, before going back to Australia a few months later, and a few stone heavier having tasted the local cider once too often over that long, hot summer.

It was after his arrival at the Australian Academy that the first of his many indiscretions arose. Once, sitting around the pool in Darwin, three young Asian girls were flashed by members of the team that Warne was playing in. Terry Jenner described it in typical Australian fashion as 'dropping yer keks and brown eyeing them', but there were serious implications, and one cannot help thinking that if authority figures had been harder on Shane, would some of his later problems in life have come to the fore?

Jenner himself was what the Aussies describe as a 'larrikin', or 'a bit of a chap', as we say here in England. He had just come out of prison for a fraud to fund his gambling habit, yet he was Warne's mentor and guru.

Warne's career is littered with indiscretions. Some of his sledging has been disgraceful over the years. As a young player, the committed Christian, South African Andrew Hudson, was shocked as, having been dismissed, Warne yelled, 'fuck off, fuck off, Hudson. Just fuck off!' He was even more surprised when Shane threw the ball back once to keeper Ian Healy, and the ball was intercepted by Hudson's wrist, fracturing it and keeping him out for two matches.

Michael Slater was supposedly a good friend and teammate, proud to wear the 'Baggy Green' with Warne, but having battled nervous and mental health problems, Slater was astounded to hear Warne and Victorian wicketkeeper Darren Berry sledging him with 'tick tock', implying that he was a walking time bomb. This was allegedly from his mate.

Matthew Sinclair, the New Zealander, was another who arrived at the crease in a Test match once to be greeted by Warne screaming, 'Fuck off, you buck-toothed fuck!'. Chatting with friends afterwards the perplexed Sinclair questioned, 'what was all that about? I know my teeth stick out a bit but I hardly know the bloke.'

Graeme Smith famously said in 2002, 'Warnie? He just stands there and calls you a c*** all day.'

Matthew Maynard was told to 'take that fucking shot back to Wales', whilst Darryl Cullinan had to visit a sports psychologist, much to the delight of the blond Victorian leg spinner. Then there was the mocking, either of an injured Chris Cairns, or the ability of No. 11 Paul Adams with the bat. Even in later years in England, when at Hampshire, Chris Adams complained that Warne had deliberately set out to humiliate one of his Sussex players in retaliation for a bit of earlier chat. Nothing was sacred to Warnie once you crossed the white line. Even his career finished with him getting fined for almost having a punch-up with Marlon Samuels in the Big Bash League.

Apart from the sledging there were the scandals. Taking money from a bookie in India, with teammate Mark Waugh, would certainly merit a much harsher sentence in this day and age from the Anti-Corruption Unit of the ICC than the slap on the wrists that they received. The two Aussies had claimed it was just for giving the bookies weather reports. Again, the story given in court that the bookie was only known to the two of them as 'John' as they received $5,000 and $4,000 each would be looked into far more deeply these days. The Australian Cricket Board were also heavily criticised about their handling of the case, when other boards around the world were being more transparent in their findings. This made Warne deeply unpopular back in his home country for a while, with banners at Adelaide saying 'I don't need money to know how hot it is today', and the Barmy Army getting involved with songs about him.

The English fans had progressed from a fiscal sledge towards him with their witty, 'He's fat, he's round, there's three dollars to the pound, Shanie Warne, Shanie Warne', to the tune of 'My Old Man's a Dustman' with:

Mark Waugh is an Aussie, He wears a baggy green hat,
And when he saw the bookie's cash, he said I'm having that.
He shared it out with Warnie, they went and had some beers,
And when the ACB found out, they covered it up for years.

Another scandal arose from a time when he was supposed to have given up smoking. Having received money for endorsing a 'non-smoking product' which helps a smoker to give up nicotine, Warne was then photographed by two schoolboys in New Zealand with a fag hanging out of his mouth. He tried to wrestle the camera from them, using threatening words towards them such as 'cockhead' and 'fuckface', so the boys claimed, and security and the police were called in yet another sensational drama.

A ban for taking illegal substances was another in a long line of misdemeanours, when he was caught taking a diuretic. A diuretic is something that is generally taken to mask the traces of another drug, perhaps taken to enhance performance. Rather than come clean to the authorities, Warne concocted some story that his mother had given it to him for weight loss, and he had just taken the tablet on a one-off basis. He claimed it was to reduce fluid, as his mother had noticed that he had a double chin in a press conference. He received a one-year ban for his troubles. Weight had often been an issue for the man whose diet consisted of toasted cheese sandwiches, pizzas, tinned spaghetti and twenty cigarettes a day.

Then there was his marriage. Simone Callaghan was a pretty promotions girl when she met Shane in the early 1990s. They married and had three children. Unfortunately, like many other cricketers, Shane struggled with his fidelity and marriage vows, and a string of women have come forward suggesting that Shane had come on to them. His media of choice seems to be the text message, and voicemails and texts sent from him to a nurse in Leicester, implying that he was on the point of orgasm, found their way into the British tabloid press.

Other stories were rife, and there were plenty of women who would be prepared to kiss and tell on the blonde Victorian. One photo, of an overweight Warne in his 'budgie smugglers' (as they say in Australia) with a couple of girls, found its way on to the Internet.

On another occasion he shared a night with two young ladies in a hotel in Kensington before heading back down to Hampshire to take seven Middlesex wickets in a resounding victory. Having patched up his marriage to Simone, he then sent a text to her which was meant for another woman and that was the final straw. The man who was a magician with a cricket ball in his hand was a complete fool with a mobile phone.

A relationship with the English model Liz Hurley followed, but even that finished towards the end of 2013 (or the beginning of 2014).

Yet Warne was an absolute genius on a cricket pitch, with a great sense of theatre. No wonder he had the nickname 'Hollywood'. He generally saved the best for England as well.

His first ball on English soil in Test cricket was termed 'the ball of the century' as it was delivered from right arm over the wicket, drifting in and pitching on leg stump before spinning sharply away, clipping the top of Mike Gatting's off bail. The Middlesex veteran was left looking dumbfounded, Graham Gooch describing it as, 'Gatt stood there looking like someone had nicked his lunch'. Either that or someone had told Gatt he had to date Rosemary Conley.

Warnie was the English nemesis, and hat-tricks to win Tests, or an 8–71 against us, made him the scourge of Englishmen throughout the 1990s and early millennium. Even his 40 wickets in vain during the 2005 English Ashes-winning series made that series far closer than it should have been, and on the last day the Barmy Army rose as one to him, chanting 'we wish you were English'.

He was no fool with the bat either, a fine slip catcher and a brilliant, thoughtful captain who, in my own personal opinion, would have made a far better skipper than Ricky Ponting. He wasn't always popular within his own dressing room, though, with Adam Gilchrist once telling a journalist in New Zealand, 'Don't worry if Warnie gets the shits with you. The rest of the team won't care, we know what he is like.'

Michael Vaughan also got stuck into him during that 2005 series, when Warne started to sledge him from slip, replying with, 'Even your teammates don't like you, so you lot are not as united as you might think you are'.

Warne has probably earned more money out of the game than anyone else in history as of early 2014, Sachin Tendulkar or MS Dhoni apart. Sponsorship deals with numerous high-profile brands such as Nike, Oakley sunglasses, 888 Poker and many more, along with newspaper columns, commentary and opinions that he was paid far more than for telling 'John' if it was going to rain or not, made him seriously wealthy. Along with playing in an era where cricketers have been paid far more than their ancestors, the contracts with Victoria, Hampshire, Rajasthan Royals and Melbourne Stars have all supplemented a very healthy central contract with the Australia team. However, he did end up with 708 Test wickets, along with a further 293 in One Day Internationals, something, supposedly, that leg spinners were too much of a luxury for.

Warne is a walking paradox. A genius, yet a fool. An overtly confident Australian with the self-doubts that wrack all of us cricketers, let alone leg spinners. Despised by many women but loved by many men, he deserves credit for changing the game of cricket. He deserves credit for enticing so many kids into wanting to bowl leg spin, one of the most beautiful yet difficult arts. He deserves credit for being around for so long, for the work he has done for charity, much of which goes unnoticed, and for keeping cricket in the headlines. He truly is a character of the game.

Just put a ball in his hand and not a mobile phone.

POSHEST CRICKET XI

Cricket is a game that attracts posh blokes. Some of these are real characters, whilst others are just plain posh, playing for fun before disappearing off to a real career in the City. The amount of red chinos I saw on offer at Lord's in May 2013 for the England v. New Zealand game, among blokes no doubt called Miles, Jeremy and Rupert, is a testament that posh blokes and cricket still go together. On the public school circuit, cricket in the summer and rugby in the winter still prevails, and I'm sure we've all played against a 'Hugo' or a 'Tarquin' somewhere along the line. Here we look at the poshest names in cricket, and pick our eleven based on the names of the finest cads, bounders and rotters ever to set foot on a cricket pitch.

COLIN INGLEBY-MACKENZIE
Educated at Eton, he was the last amateur to captain Hampshire and he led them to the title in 1961 due to some bold declarations, and the promise 'that his team were in bed before breakfast'! One of the last people to see Lord Lucan, Ingleby-Mackenzie became President of the MCC. Proper posh.

RORY HAMILTON-BROWN
Educated at Millfield, this chap was equally talented on the rugger and cricket pitch, and was courted by Harlequins before deciding that his talents lay in cricket. Rory moved between Sussex and Surrey twice; this man's chauffeur must know the A23 intimately.

ASHLEY HARVEY-WALKER

Born with the riff-raff in East Ham, this bloke represented
Derbyshire in the 1970s. An interesting character, this
joker actually gave umpire Dickie Bird his false teeth in the
snow-affected game at Buxton in 1975. He was tragically
murdered in a Johannesburg bar in 1997, when a double-barrelled
shotgun ended the double-barrelled surnamed, all-rounder's life.

JOHN ROBERT TROUTBECK BARCLAY

Anyone with the name Troutbeck has to make our side, and this
Old Etonian is a fan of The Middle Stump on Twitter these days!
Now President of the MCC, he was a fine skipper of Sussex
back in the 1980s and there are many japes and stories involving
this man over the years. Whether Barclay banks at Barclays,
who knows? We think Coutts is more his style.

DOUGLAS JARDINE

So posh he was even rumoured to get out of the bath to pee!
Jardine was hated in Australia due to his bodyline tactics in 1933
and was a bounder, cad and a rotter all in one, according to
those Down Under. A bloody fine skipper though, Jardine could
only have played for Surrey. Less Kennington, more Kensington.

THE NAWAB OF PATAUDI

Now this bloke is taking it to a different level. Not just content with being posh, this geezer was more or less a prince. Indian royalty. Educated at Winchester School, he was national champion at that well-known sport of the common man, rackets. After this, he scored a shed load for Sussex before his tragic accident, where he lost his eye. Too posh for a glass one, his replacement was made from opaque crystal.

OLiVER HANNON-DALBY

Must be the poshest-named bloke ever to come from Halifax. Rumour reaches us that, since this chap joined Warwickshire from Yorkshire in 2013, the players are too posh to go to the gym any more, and instead use the 'James'!

TOBiAS SKELTON ROLAND-JONES

An ex-pupil of Hampton School, this Middlesex chap chose the lure of Lord's to ply his trade after growing up in the Surrey championship in club cricket. This seamer has no need to bowl into the rough, and will no doubt be the poshest-named bloke to play for England in the future, as he has made an outstanding start to his professional career.

EBONY-JEWEL CORA-LEE CAMELLIA ROSAMOND RAINFORD-BRENT

This lady, who has represented England on numerous occasions, was apparently christened after a few disputes when she was the only girl born with three older brothers, and the multitude of names appeased everyone. An even posher name to grace the ladies' game than Rachael Heyhoe Flint, all scorers are relieved that she never batted much with Chaminda Vaas!

MICHAEL FIELD-BUSS

This bloke played for the not-so-posh counties of Essex and Nottinghamshire in the 1980s and 1990s, and had a decent career before packing up in 1995. Asked once what his favourite game was, he replied, 'partridge, but I'm partial to grouse in season'.

VASBERT CONNIEL DRAKES

What a name and what a player too. This guy should have played a lot more for the West Indies. The chilled out Drakes was one of only four batsmen to be given out 'timed out', and even more unusually he was on board a flight to South Africa when it happened! First class we hope, Vas?

TWELFTH MAN

Not overtly posh in terms of double-barrelledness, but I seem to remember an opening bat who was certainly playing for Cambridge University a few years ago called Quentin Cake, which suggests a straw boater worn at a rakish angle and at least three times too many teeth in the upper jaw. The thought of Quentin punting along the Cam, quaffing Bollinger (the champagne, not Doug) with a couple of fillies by the name of Henrietta and Ophelia in tow springs to mind. Saying that, I have never seen the bloke.

TANGO

Steve Kirby is a shining light in the modern game. Not just because of his flame hair that makes him stand out amongst the crowd, but because he is one of the characters of the game, in an era when the media-trained youngsters give monotone interviews. 'Kirbs' is most definitely not that man.

He comes with a reputation. I am lucky enough to have got to know him over the past few years and I was, in truth, frankly crapping myself before interviewing him, thinking that the man you see on the cricket pitch would be the man I was interviewing. How wrong was I? He is without a doubt one of the nicest people on the circuit, a gentleman, and an example to any young cricketer who never gives up. In addition, he has helped out the charity Melanoma UK (who will benefit from the sale of this book) in many ways unnoticed, not being one to brag, and having had a close scare a few years ago.

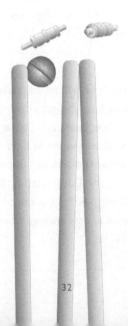

Born in Bury on the outskirts of Manchester, he first played for Leicestershire before being released, and found a living selling industrial flooring. It was only a call from Yorkshire – who handed him a debut in 2001 – that saved his career and, filling in for Matthew Hoggard who was away on England duty, Tango grabbed his chance with both hands, picking up 7 wickets. A couple of games later, 12 wickets in the match against his former employers at Leicestershire made the country sit up and take notice, and his 47 wickets that year at a shade over 20 apiece was one of the reasons why the holy grail of the County Championship returned to Yorkshire after a long absence. The irony of someone born over the Pennines in Lancashire spearheading them to the title didn't matter a jot to even the most die-hard Yorkshire member, as they had a new hero at Headingley.

A trip to the England Academy beckoned and, although he has been one of the best fast bowlers in the country for a number of years, and despite inclusion on a few occasions in the England Lions side, Kirbs has never quite made full international honours.

It was during this time with Yorkshire that many stories began to go around the cricketing grapevine about the ginger haired firebrand. He famously told Mike Atherton that he had seen 'better batters in a fish and chip shop', as he dismissed him twice in a game. In Kirbs' words to me, 'Athers couldn't wait to get away from me. He must have thought, "Who is this ginger haired lunatic?"' The ex-England skipper promptly retired after that game as well.

On another occasion, he was once fired up in a Roses game and, fed up with Chris Schofield scoring forty-odd runs off him, all behind square, Kirbs turned to the umpire and said, 'I'm going around the wicket, and call an ambulance'. The umpire could hardly believe his ears and asked him to repeat it, so Kirbs said, 'Right arm around the wicket, and call a fucking ambulance!' After much laughter from Chris Silverwood and Ryan Sidebottom, the sightscreens were moved and Kirby charged in and bowled a bouncer. Headingley, never being the quickest track on the circuit, allowed the Lancastrian to pull Steve for 6 on to the Western terrace, where an old bloke was dozing in the sun after his lunch. The ball hit him flush on top of the head, so they ended up calling an ambulance after all!

He wasn't all bad though. A great believer in having a beer after the game, he is one of the most popular players on the circuit and his persona off the pitch is vastly different from the bloke who crosses the white line. Kirbs bemoans the fact that modern-day teams dash off straight away, as people now don't get to know or understand the characters, and so then take them for who the on-field person seems to be.

The way he is can go against him too, and once, playing on a quick deck at Chester-le-Street he was facing a fired-up Shoaib Akhtar. Kirbs hadn't said a word when batting, but Nicky Peng of Durham, fielding at short leg, decided to wind up his quick bowler and motivate him at Tango's expense. Peng screamed out, 'You'll never believe what he just called you Shoaib, the Rawalpindi tuk-tuk,' when Kirbs hadn't said a word. The Yorkshire bowler was telling Peng to shut up when the 'Rawalpindi Express' let a beamer go vaguely in the direction of Steve's head. A massive hoo-ha erupted and eventually the game continued. The next ball was the quickest bouncer ever, according to Kirbs, and went for 4 byes over the head of Phil Mustard, the Durham keeper, before hitting the sightscreen and bouncing all the way back.

Another infamous story goes around about Kirbs, when he was selected for a charity fashion show. The catwalk and ginger-haired quick bowlers are two things that aren't often put together, and Kirbs' stage fright was quelled by downing a bottle of wine. Unfortunately this came back to bite him as he got to the end of his parade, turned and promptly fell off the stage, grabbing the first thing to hand – a brand new £8,000 plasma television, which came crashing down with Kirbs, to much laughter from his teammates and the audience.

A legend down at Somerset now, Kirbs' reputation hasn't got him into too much trouble over the years. His language and gestures, calls for the emergency services and other rhetoric has pushed him close to the mark, but, apart from an incident at Gloucestershire for rolling a ball across a car park, he has never been up before the beak.

He will go down as a man who has worked extremely hard at his game, an honest one who has added value to English cricket over the years, and for that he should be applauded. He never gave up, from when he was a kid and released by Leicestershire, to battling injury all of those years later at Somerset, and he famously told me, 'without wanting to sound like Martin Luther King, if you have a dream … go for it'. I have been lucky enough to get to know Kirbs in recent months, having done a gig with him in Leeds, and he is one of the nicest blokes around. He just doesn't have a bad word to say about anyone, and he has time for all cricket fans. The man is a true superstar in my eyes and I won't have a bad word said about him.

What the future holds for Steve Kirby, God knows, but he is a legend down at Taunton. Loved by the people, the last couple of years have been dogged by injuries. He would be fantastic in the media, and his stories, his anecdotes and his take on the game of cricket are well worth listening to. As he once told me, 'Anything where I have a beer in my hand and talk shit with people. I'm good at that.'

Steve Kirby is good at a lot of things, and when he retires not only cricket but I will miss him.

THE MASTER OF SLEDGING

Many things have been written about Steve Waugh. A fine player, a fine competitor, a fine captain, a decent all-rounder, but to me he was probably the hardest man ever to set foot on a cricket pitch. He made the Aussies into a machine. Yes, Border and Simpson started it, and Mark Taylor continued it, but for me, Steve Waugh took them to a level that no side in Test cricket had ever been to. The West Indies of the 1970s and 1980s were brutal, but this lot raised the bar.

It is easy when you have two of the finest bowlers that have ever lived in your team, such as Glenn McGrath and Shane Warne, but Waugh instilled a steeliness into the Baggy Greens that hadn't been seen before. Paul Nixon says in his book *Keeping Quiet* that he first came across Waugh at the end of the 1980s. After attempting two sweeps that he missed, Waugh piped up with 'Fuck me mate, what time does the cricket start?' The two became the best of friends when they played together at Kent.

Waugh wouldn't back down from anybody – even the 6ft 9in Curtly Ambrose, who he asked, 'What the fuck are you looking at?' When Ambrose replied, 'Don't cuss me, man', 'Tugga', as the Aussie was known, told him to go and 'get fucked', causing the nearest thing that I have ever seen to a punch-up on a cricket pitch.

Waugh liked to call his sledging 'mental disintegration' and would always select somebody before a series to target. Glenn McGrath would often back him up.

Waugh played Worcestershire over here in 1997, and in his book wrote that the Worcester player David Leatherdale 'wouldn't get a bowl in a Chinese restaurant', despite taking 5–10 against the tourists. Waugh then visited the ground on the banks of the River Severn on the 2001 tour and, even before he had faced a ball, the slip cordon were asking him if he would like 'sweet and sour with his guard'. Having played and missed, one wag asked him 'if he had swallowed a fortune cookie'. Waugh, unfazed, still managed to grind out a score as the orders for crispy aromatic duck, beef in black bean sauce and sesame prawn toast continued from the hosts.

Steve Waugh was well known for his harsh demeanour in his own country. Once, when taking guard in a Sheffield Shield game for New South Wales, Waugh took an eternity, had a look around, re-took his guard, had another look, counted the fielders before the comment came from Victorian Jamie Siddons at slip, 'Come on mate, this isn't a fucking Test match, we haven't got all day'. Quick as a flash, Waugh responded with 'Of course not mate, you're here'! Saying that, the story of whether he said 'Mate, you have just dropped the World Cup' to Herschelle Gibbs is rumoured not to be true.

It was this sort of mindset that led Waugh to become the No. 1 batsman in the world and finish up with close to 11,000 Test runs in a career that spanned eighteen years and 168 Test matches. I wouldn't say he was the most talented batsman to have played the game, yet his flintiness and hardness took him to a level that only the greats of the game have achieved.

Waugh also led his team to sixteen consecutive victories, breaking the record of the West Indies, who had previously held it with eleven. He seemed to delight in breaking the Windies, as his three consecutive bouncers to Viv Richards in 1986 showed; a statement against the barrage that sides had received for years previously.

Waugh was more than just a hard man, though. He encouraged sides to look at other aspects of life and not just cricket. He made his side visit Gallipoli, the scene of the massacre of thousands of Australian and New Zealand (ANZAC) troops in the First World War, whilst over here on tour in the UK. Waugh also raised hundreds of thousands for children with leprosy in India, and his work today still continues with the Steve Waugh Foundation.

Waugh was famous for the slog sweep, and right to the end of his career, the verbals continued. In his last Test match he went out to bat and 19-year-old Indian wicketkeeper Parthiv Patel said to him, 'Come on, let's see that slog sweep one last time,' referring to his trademark risky shot. Waugh responded simply with, 'Have some fucking respect, you were in nappies when I started my career'.

Steve Waugh, hard, ballsy and gimlet-eyed to the end.

THE PRINCE OF WALES

In July 2013, I was doing a book signing in Cardiff at the SWALEC, as Glamorgan hosted Somerset in front of 9,000 partisan fans full of beer and what the Welsh call *hywl*, on a hot summer's night. I was approached by a gentleman who was obviously from the valleys and had an extremely strong accent, who asked me what the book was about. I told him it was a selection of stories from the game, along with interviews with players. I then went on to tell him that there were a few interviews with Glamorgan connections. I threw out the names of current opener Gareth Rees and ex-players and now journalists, Steve James and Mike Selvey, and the bloke didn't move a muscle (no offence to those fine gentlemen). I then said Jason Gillespie, one of Glamorgan's favourite overseas players and a member of probably the finest team to ever set foot on a cricket pitch; Australia that is, and not Glamorgan. Still not a twitch, before finally I laid my trump card. I said, 'Oh yeah and Matthew Maynard as well', and quick as a flash his eyes opened wide, a huge grin appeared across his face and he bought a signed copy.

Maynard has been loved in Wales since bursting on to the scene with an amazing hundred at Swansea in 1985. On a ground which has gone down in folklore for six-hitting after Garfield Sobers' feat in 1968, this debutant pulled off an amazing act. How many other 19 year olds would slap three consecutive sixes to reach a hundred? You could tell then that he had something special about him.

A year later he was the youngest Glamorgan player to reach 1,000 runs, and a Test debut followed against the West Indies in 1988. Unfortunately he could not transfer his vast talent on to the international stage, and after playing against the 1989 touring Australians, announced that he would be going on the rebel tour of South Africa. South Africa is a part of the world Maynard was always drawn to, and even attended a stag do there once with a friend of his in Kwe Kwe, formerly known as Que Que, over the border in Zimbabwe, where his friend apparently ate a pig's penis, so Matt tells me.

Domestic runs followed aplenty, before a century before lunch against the 1993 Australians led to a Test recall against them at the Oval. I was lucky enough to attend that day, but Maynard told me later that it was during this game that there was a sledge which absolutely threw him completely as he was walking out to bat.

En route to the wicket, there was an aeroplane circling over the Oval, no doubt waiting to land at Heathrow, where most planes arriving from the east follow the route of the River Thames. Shane Warne pointed up to it and said, 'you'd best get some runs mate, or you won't be getting on one of those this winter'. Apparently it just completely ruined the concentration of the Welshman, although he did find himself on that plane after all, to the Caribbean. It was here that he was hit in the throat by Devon Malcolm, batting on a dodgy surface in an under-prepared net, when none of the other England batsmen fancied giving the bowler a workout-cum-fitness-test. Maynard joked with me that his days of being head chorister in the Bangor Cathedral Choir were over at that point.

The Glamorgan captaincy arrived in 1995, and Maynard brought home the bacon by steering his side to victory in the County Championship in 1997. The holy grail of trophies, this cemented the love affair of the South Welsh with this son of Anglesey. The Manic Street Preachers, who were a huge band at the time and also hailing from the principality, filled their dressing room with champagne, and stories of that night have become the stuff of legend. One of the biggest hits of that year was their 'Design for Life' and on the B-side they had a track called 'Mr Carbohydrate'. One of the lyrics in there is, 'Have you heard of Matthew Maynard, He's my favourite cricketer, I'd rather watch him bat, than pick up my guitar'.

He was named as one of *Wisden*'s five cricketers of the year in 1998, before leading Glammy to Lord's in 2000 as one last finale on the international stage occurred. Unfortunately for Maynard, he still couldn't transfer his magic on to the big stage, and he went into coaching before becoming an assistant to Duncan Fletcher. The charisma of Maynard, allied to the astute brain of the quieter Fletcher, was supposed to have been a major factor in helping England win the 2005 Ashes, but it was not without some controversy. Public challenges from another Fletcher – Essex man Keith – about Maynard's excessive partying, along with Mike Atherton regarding his South African connections during apartheid, didn't deter the Glamorgan man from doing a fine job for his country, as he rammed their words back down their throats in the best way possible.

If Maynard's considerable talent had not delivered the goods for England on the pitch, he had done so off the pitch. He then went out to South Africa, winning lots of silverware for Nashua Titans, and has the respect of many fine players, some describing him as the best coach in the world. In an area of the globe which has produced elite coaches such as Duncan Fletcher, Graeme Ford, Andy Flower, Ray Jennings and Gary Kirsten, this is some accolade indeed.

I had the privilege of chatting with Maynard in an interview at the end of May 2012. Sadly, this was just three weeks before the tragic death of his son, Tom, who was no doubt destined to be an even better player than Matthew. I had also interviewed Tom on 2 April 2012, just over two months before his untimely passing at the age of just 23.

I found both of the Maynards to be lovely people, especially Matthew. More than happy to chat with me for nearly an hour, we discussed North Wales, with my family roots coming from Penmaenmawr, whilst he grew up in a pub in Menai Bridge just over the Menai Strait in Anglesey. We discussed Manchester City and the legendary drinking ability of Jason Gillespie, who Maynard described as a 'decent swiller'. He gave me lots of time, and didn't think himself too big to be interviewed by a start-up cricket blog. He was humorous, genuine and warm, yet discussed the complexities of the game in depth, and I came off the phone with the utmost respect and time for the man.

Therefore I was absolutely stunned and devastated when I heard the news on the lunchtime of 18 June 2012. I sat in silence for ages and cried. I cried for Tom, cried for the family and for Matthew, who had been so vibrant during that interview, and then cried even more when I read the touching and heart-tugging piece written by Steve James regarding Tom in the *Telegraph* the following day. The whole of cricket had been touched by the tragedy, and I wasn't alone in my tears. There were those far closer to him who have struggled with their recovery to this day. I never really even knew Tom, I'd just spoken with him and his father in the preceding months, and found them to be both funny, entertaining and kind. However, it hit something inside of me, and in a way has made me closer to my own children. I don't know how I would ever cope being in that situation, and I am not sure anyone would until it has happened to them.

The way Matt conducted himself during the aftermath of something that no parent wishes ever to have to go through has been commendable and he is now a leading light in the charitable trust designed to help future starlets of the game, named after his son, the Tom Maynard Trust. The trust has raised funds with high-profile bike rides, cross-Channel swims and various other events, many of which have included some of the biggest names in the game. Matthew is selflessly ensuring that the memory of Tom lives on, and the legacy is left to the sport.

Maynard has also returned part-time to Glamorgan to help out, and they will be better for the experience. What the future holds for this character of cricket I don't know, but one thing is for certain – he will be adored by his people over the other side of the Severn Bridge. Over 40,000 runs has seen to that, and in that part of the world they adore their sportsmen, either with a willow or a rugby ball in their hand.

Arise, the Prince of Wales.

THE CROWDS

Cricket crowds have long made an atmosphere at a cricket ground. Whether it is at Test match, county or even club level, the crowd can give the place at atmospheric buzz. I had been to Lord's as a kid with my Somerset-supporting uncle George, and I will never forget the amount of pissed people I witnessed that day. Hundreds upon hundreds of pissed-up gentlemen who had all travelled down the M4, with cider their fuel for the day.

My next recollection was as a 14 year old at Lord's, having bunked the day off school I went to watch the One Day International between England and the West Indies in 1984. It was in the days when you could sit on the grass between the stands and the boundary rope, and one gentleman of a Rastafarian persuasion next to me was smoking Moroccan Marlboros all day.

Another chap next to me downed a bottle of Captain Morgan rum along with a good eight cans of Red Stripe, whilst proceeding to blow into a conch shell for most of the day. His tobacco with which he made his cigarettes seemed to be greener than a Headingley wicket in April, too. The banter, the verbals, the jerk chicken and the music kept coming all day.

At one point Greenidge hit one that bounced just short of the boundary rope and nearly killed me as it whistled past my ear. The man from St Peter, in Barbados, was pretty close to making me visit St Peter upstairs, although it wasn't enough for one wag in the crowd behind us, who shouted, 'Cuthbert man, you got no power dese days. That would have gone for six a few years back, man', to much raucous laughter. He seemed to delight in using the full name of players and most of his piss-taking was reserved for his own side. Larry Gomes copped unbelievable amounts of stick, with him yelling, 'Hilary, you should get lots of runs today boy, dis is your home ground', in reference to Gomes' unsuccessful season at Lord's in 1975.

Even at club level, a West Indian chap at a club in Enfield regularly winds up our opening bowlers. When one of their batsmen hits a boundary he will yell out, 'Put de rubbish in de bin!'

It's not just here, though. The Caribbean is an outstanding place to watch cricket, and the locals know how to have fun. The much missed St John's Recreation Ground in Antigua was a superb venue. Not only did it have the residents of the prison next door helping out to do the pitch, but the backdrop of Chicky the DJ spinning the tunes whilst cross-dressing Gravy danced on the podium made this a surreal venue. Chuck in the fact that it was a shirt front of a pitch, and Lara would help himself as regularly as the all-inclusive holidaymakers to this island, and you could see why the locals loved this temple, where they paid homage to Andy Roberts, King Vivi and Curtly Ambrose.

The Trini Posse Stand, situated roughly around square leg at Queen's Park Oval, is also not for the faint hearted. Back in the day you could pay $20 to sit there all day and 'lime'. 'Liming' is having a good time, and the music, beers, food and pretty girls are there all day, whilst many a broken body can be surveyed after play has ended. Apparently it was dreamed up by a dentist, although with this being the venue that England were skittled for 46 once, it has been as painful as root canal surgery for those from these shores.

Sabina Park was another in these islands which could get lively, especially when Michael Holding was getting it through past people's noses.

Other countries also have crowds which can get boisterous, to say the least. Bay 13 at Melbourne was always a part of the ground in front of which no England fielder enjoyed having to go down. It was always famous for helping out with the choreography of Merv Hughes' warm-ups.

The Hill at Sydney, now long gone, was another place which saw its fair share of bad behaviour. Always the cheapest part of the ground to get into, the advent of One Day cricket in the 1970s saw this place turn out like a cricketing Magaluf. Cold beers, 'eskies', fights and boorish behaviour were the norm, and they had to put a stop to the sales of alcohol here.

South Africa has some great crowds too. The variation of crowds here is symbolic of the various types of population in this Rainbow Nation, and the Afrikaans community at the partisan

Pretoria are a very different crowd from the Indian-loving fans in diverse Durban. Port Elizabeth, with the brass band striking up hymns such as 'Kum ba Ya' is a wonderful place, and the knowledgeable patrons of Newlands, at Cape Town, add to this beautiful venue with the dramatic Table Mountain as a backdrop. Jo'burg, with the Bull Ring, can be hostile, especially with a fired-up Allan Donald bowling there.

India has some wonderful support, and the IPL has brought joyous crowds to our television screens in the UK. The worship of Sachin – especially at the wonderfully named Wankhede Stadium in Mumbai – could get oppressive, as could the heat in Chennai. Eden Garden in Kolkata would regularly get over 100,000 people a day packing in there, although when India started losing in the semi-final of the World Cup in 1996, it got even warmer as a few of the locals set fire to the place, causing the game to be abandoned.

Fruit being thrown at visiting players can also be a regular occurrence, although Phil DeFreitas was none too impressed once when a 10in, spiked metal object came whistling past his ear.

Even at home, crowds can be diverse across the country and there are plenty of characters. Graeme Fowler said that spending the day on the boundary at Scarborough as a Lancastrian wasn't much fun, and the Western Terrace at Headingley saw many a beer sunk. Fancy dress was the order of the day here for Test matches, and with Darren Gough playing up to them, this was a venue which got more audible as the day went on. What would start out in a genteel fashion would then start picking up by 2 or 3 in the afternoon and by 5 p.m., it would be like the Ministry of Sound.

Edgbaston is another one where it can get lively, and the old Rea Bank used to rock once the Brummies had sunk a few 'sherbets'. Taunton, when the locals have a few ciders down them, can be a cacophony of 'Wurzel' laughter, while there are always wags and comedians at Trent Bridge.

Chelmsford can be partisan, especially for T20, and Canterbury can get going when they have been on the Spitfire. Old Trafford is another, whilst at Leicester they miss the much-loved West Indian, Lewis Springett, who died a few years back. His cries of 'Leave the gate open, he'll be back in a minute' as the opposition batsman walked out to bat or 'Brandy time' are heard no more. Even the bacon-and-egg tie brigade at Lord's make the venue in their own idiosyncratic way, whilst over the Thames at the ground all Middlesex fans refer to as 'the Gasworks', the Oval is a completely different atmosphere.

On my only visit to Cardiff for a T20 game, it was full of groups, especially groups of lads, all enjoying themselves, downing beer like there was no tomorrow and the local pubs, such as *Y Mochyn Du* (The Black Pig) outside the ground, were heaving. They love their cricket down there.

Some say a county cricket ground is like a dyslexic using Twitter – 140 strange characters not making much sense. There is far more to a cricket crowd than that.

So, whether it is just in the United Kingdom or whether it is a worldwide phenomenon, cricket crowds can be diverse and interesting. Crowds make the venue, and enhance the experience of a day out at the cricket. From Kennington to Kingston, and from Melbourne to Manchester, the crowds are very much characters of cricket.

THE BEARDED XI

Having watched the fantastic Somerset v. Warwickshire game on Sky TV in 2013, it struck me that the stand-out performers on each side both sported facial fuzz. Rikki Clarke, for Warwickshire, and Jack Leach of Somerset both sported beards, and later on I watched a documentary about the 1981 Ashes. You could pick a team just from the players on show in that to be honest. Numerous cricketers have beards these days, and not just the hirsute heroes below. Here is my finest Bearded XI:

MiKE BREARLEY - CAPTAiN
Brearley was christened 'the Ayatollah' on the 1978–79 tour of Australia. The finest skipper of my generation, and possibly ever, although some say he wasn't worth his place in the side.

W.G. GRACE
The Bristolian doctor was just as famous for his beard as he was for his batting. Rumours that when he was a younger man he asked Mrs Grace to do a handstand naked to see what it would look like before he grew one are unfounded.

HASHiM AMLA
No side would be complete without Hashim Amla. A man who looks like his head is upside down, his chin is the most overgrown thing since Terry Waite's allotment back in the early 1990s.

MiKE GATTiNG
Gatting prefers just the goatee these days, as opposed to the full frontal he sported in his playing days. Often the lunches were so good at Lord's that Gatt would hide Nancy's spotted dick in his beard so he could have a mid-session snack!

ALLAN BORDER

Nicknamed 'Herbie' from 'herbaceous border', the Aussie captain regularly went for the 'tash' look as favoured by the Liverpool football teams, or the 'tash and beard', as worn by Kenny Everett at the time.

IAN BOTHAM

No side would be complete without Beefy *c.* 1981, destroying the Aussies. No finer sight greets an Englishman than the old pics of 'Both' – long-sleeved jumper with his mandible mane, thrashing the old enemy all around Headingley.

MATT PRIOR

Makes our team just ahead of Rodney Marsh, the Aussie keeper, that is, and not the old Man City and QPR player. He modelled himself on the old Indian wicketkeeper Syed Kirmani – they both prefer to grow hair on their chins as opposed to the top of their heads.

GRAEME BEARD

Not sure if he ever grew a beard, to be honest, but seeing as he was on tour with the 1981 Aussies, he no doubt had one. No wonder it took the Old Bill so long to catch the Yorkshire Ripper with so many players sporting beards from this era. Everyone must have been a suspect, apart from Kim Hughes.

CHRIS OLD

The man known as 'Chilly' because his name was C. Old. He was often injured when clean shaven. Once he sported half an ounce of Old Holborn on his chin, he hit one of the quickest hundreds of all time.

MiKE HENDRiCK

The spitting image of the man from the *Joy of Sex* manual, this man was responsible for the boom in birth rates in Derbyshire throughout the early 1980s. An unlucky bowler, it is without a shadow of doubt that the 'Hendo' lookalike from the *Joy of Sex* had far more luck in his partner's corridor of uncertainty than the Derbyshire and England seamer did in the corridor of uncertainty just outside off stump.

MUSHTAQ AHMED

Only in the modern game could a man have his beard sponsored by Adidas. Mushy's three-striped beard was responsible for many a wicket, having dazzled the batsman with his leg spin.

Moeen Ali, aka 'the beard that's feared', Jason Gillespie, Liam Plunkett, Rikki Clarke, Saeed Anwar, Navjot Singh Sidhu, Bishen Bedi, Sir Vivian Richards, Michael Holding, Martin Kent, Ray Bright, Peter Willey, Geoff Humpage, Alan Butcher, Graham Barlow, Mike Selvey, Monty Panesar and any English player who toured India in the 1980s can all be considered very unlucky they didn't make the (razor) cut!

WE NEED TO TALK ABOUT KEVIN

Kevin Pietersen is a man who has polarised opinions ever since he started playing cricket. Born in Pietermaritzburg in June 1980 to an English mother and a South African father, 'KP', as he is commonly known, made his debut for his native Natal before making his displeasure known regarding the racial quota system in South Africa. This is a system that, regardless of how good a player is, there has to be a quota of people from varying ethnic backgrounds within that team. It is a sad indictment of a country that has been through the discriminatory politics of apartheid.

Nasser Hussein, then England captain, said after a warm-up game on the tour to South Africa against Kwazulu Natal:

> Their young off-spinner plonked himself down in our changing room after the game, and asked if I knew of any English clubs that I could fix him up with. I gave him my brother Mel's number as I thought he might be quite useful for Fives & Heronians, in the Essex League, but it turned out that he had bigger ambitions than that.

Originally an off-spinner who could bat a bit, his batting got better and better and, after four years of playing for Nottinghamshire under the tutelage of Clive Rice, and qualifying for England via his mother's nationality, KP made his England debut versus Zimbabwe in a One Day International. Having smashed the South Africans in South Africa in the same format, whilst receiving the sort of abuse that would equip him well for an Ashes series against Shane Warne and Glenn McGrath, Pietersen made his Test debut at Lord's, replacing Graham Thorpe.

He batted well in a losing cause, top scoring in both innings, and showed positivity in smiting Shane Warne for a huge six into the top of the Mound Stand, that emulated that team's positive spirit throughout the series. The need to score quickly and match the Aussies was the key to winning that series, and in Vaughan and Trescothick, England had quick scorers. Now Pietersen came in and scored even quicker.

In what was probably the best series of all time, KP, with his skunk hairstyle (one that surely he regrets now, no doubt), saved the deciding Test at the Oval in a knock of sheer brilliance. A brave and crucial knock, England were trying to save the game, and despite being dropped by Shane Warne, his 158 was an innings of attitude and bottle. Brett Lee came steaming in at him, and KP kept taking him on and depositing him into the crowd for six. It was Test cricket at its absolute best. England won the Ashes and KP was the rising star.

Gimmicks followed, such as trying to hit a cricket ball across the River Thames, as did sponsorship deals with the likes of Red Bull, although if anyone has seen his suicidal running trying to get off the mark, maybe Pro Plus would be better rather than the adrenalin rush of Red Bull?

KP was hot property and already an integral part of the side. He joined Hampshire but such was the England side's reliance on him that he only played one game for them between 2005 and 2010. He married the pop star Jessica Taylor from the band Liberty X, with Darren Gough as his best man. He was the fastest English batsman to various milestones, and topped the ICC One Day International rankings in 2007. After twenty-five Test matches, only Don Bradman had scored more runs than him in the history of the game. The *Times* described him as, 'the most complete batsman in world cricket', whilst the *Guardian* quoted, 'England's greatest modern batsman'.

Although he was in the side that lost 5–0 in the Ashes under Andrew Flintoff, KP did well again, and even traded it with Shane Warne. At one point Warne threw a ball at him, which Pietersen hit to the boundary.

In 2008, he became England captain but, following a number of rows and disagreements with Peter Moores, he resigned after just 3 Tests and nine ODIs. Moores was relieved of his duties the same day. His relationship with the ECB never fully recovered from this, and it was the stick that was used to beat him when further controversies occurred later in his career.

In the 2009 Ashes he again had a decent series but problems with his Achilles hampered him, before he was imperious as England collected their first silverware on the world stage in One Day cricket in 2010.

The T20 World Cup was KP's crowning moment, and he was named 'Man of the Tournament' for averaging 62. The 2010 Ashes brought more runs and his 227 in Adelaide was a knock to behold.

In 2012 it all started to go a bit wrong, though. The Headingley Test against South Africa was controversial in that Pietersen was alleged to have sent texts to the other team. Some say they called Andrew Strauss a 'doos', which is Afrikaans for a box. It is also a vulgar term for the female genitalia, although Strauss was later to drop the 'c-bomb' live on air in July 2014 regarding Kevin. Both parties have apologised for their behaviour. Pietersen was then left out of the side for the third Test before being reintegrated for the tour of India.

Thank God he was, because his innings in Mumbai was one of the finest that I have seen from an Englishman. Gooch at Headingley in 1991, and KP's very own 158 in 2005 were maybe better, but this was a classy knock from a quality player. He again contributed when the Ashes were held at home in England before the tour to Australia. This was full of acrimony and finger pointing, with KP getting the blame for most of it despite being top run-scorer in the series, and England were whitewashed 5–0.

KP has always been forthright and says what he thinks. On a tour when Swann retired, Trott went home with mental health issues, Flower retired, and Cook almost lost his job, Pietersen was dropped for the tour to the Caribbean, despite being the top scorer. In a team meeting which was 'open house' and designed to be honest, Pietersen was to pay the ultimate price for being too honest and speaking the truth. Not too much is really known regarding this tour, as the finer details are subject to a severance agreement, although with his book due out in October 2014, you will probably know by the time you read this.

It was an extremely sad end to a fine player, and in my view, he deserved better. It reminded me of the end of Gower, and his celebrity friend Piers Morgan, in an interview with me in March 2014, was scathing in his attacks on certain members of the touring party.

Pietersen should be lauded as one of the finest players that I have ever seen. His switch hit and flamingo shot brought new and innovative aspects to this wonderful game, and he broke barriers year after year. No one, at the time of writing this, has scored more international runs for England. His celebrity friendships with the likes of Piers Morgan and Shane Warne have helped to promote cricket and, despite being labelled by many as a troublemaker in the dressing room, are we as a nation strong enough to exile him?

Throw in the fact that he was a decent fielder and picked up wickets with his off-spin, Pietersen should be an integral part of English cricket.

Like him or loathe him – and you will be in one camp or the other as not many are ambivalent about him – KP is most definitely a character of the game, and one who should be applauded for what he contributed to our national team for nearly a decade, not vilified – and sadly there are a few out there who still do.

MAD MERV HUGHES

Mervyn Gregory Hughes looked more like a gentleman who would frequent leather-fetish clubs in the Earl's Court area of London than an Australian fast bowler, but he was one of the best of his time, and part of the reason that the Australian team was transformed under the tutelage of Bobby Simpson and Allan Border.

With his handlebar moustache, the big Victorian had a mincing run-up of numerous small steps, but was a relatively brisk customer once he let go of the cherry. He became a god to his countrymen, a fearsome sledger and an instantly recognisable cricketer, just when the game was starting to change.

Hughes had a stint with Essex in 1983, before his Test debut in 1986. It was against the might of the West Indies that he came to prominence though, with a hat-trick over two days and 3 separate overs.

In Perth, in 1988–89, he removed Curtly Ambrose with the last ball of his 36th over, before taking out No. 11, Patrick Patterson, with the first ball of his 37th. He then trapped Gordon Greenidge lbw, first ball in the second innings to grab his hat-trick amidst raucous celebrations.

Hughes was a top man on the verbals front. He was once called a 'fat bus conductor' by Javed Miandad, before removing him a couple of balls later, running past him and shouting 'Tickets please!' He would regularly tell Graeme Hick that the instructions were on the other side of his bat when batting, and even in adversity he could still be amusing. Having once been on the end of some serious punishment in the Caribbean from Viv Richards, where the Antiguan had taken him for 4 boundaries in 1 over, Merv let out an audible fart before telling the dumbfounded Richards, 'Let's see you hit that one to the boundary'.

On another occasion, he told Robin Smith he couldn't bat, before a trademark Smith square-cut crashed the Aussie pace man to the boundary. Smith retorted with, 'What a great pair we make, hey? I can't fucking bat, and you can't fucking bowl'.

Hughes' verbals did get him into trouble on frequent occasions, and the tour in the early 1990s to South Africa was awash with bad behaviour. Having been fined $400 for telling Gary Kirsten that he was a 'weak little prick', the ACB decided to multiply the fine by ten times the amount, as it had been the third time in 15 Tests that Hughes had crossed the disciplinary tightrope. With the ink not even dry on the cheque that he had written out, a spectator abused and spat at him, causing Merv to bash the cage, screaming, 'Mate, if you have something to say, let's have it right now,' before following it up with 'You're like everyone else I have met out here, you're as weak as piss'. Naturally this cost young Mervyn another $2,000 and made him sign a good behaviour bond.

Saying that, Merv could bowl and he led the Australian attack admirably in England in 1993, where the crowds would yell 'Sumo' at him. A haul of 212 Test wickets in 53 Tests is decent by anyone's standards.

Merv then became a selector, and in his little round spectacles looked the antithesis of a fast bowler. He still tells some hilarious stories about his career. He was loved by the fans during his career and regularly you would see the Aussie fans do the 'Merv gymnastics' as they would copy his warm-ups in the crowd.

Loved by all, he really was a proper character in this game of ours.

THE FIGHTERS

Cricket, they say, is a game for gentlemen. However, under the surface people want to win, and the verbals have increased over the last thirty or so years. One of the reasons for this is money, or sides just being more desperate to win. Another thought is that perhaps because the chances of physical retribution are so slim in cricket, the verbals tend to increase. Do you think that the likes of Justin Langer would have dished out the verbals to Curtly if he were playing rugby or football? I doubt it.

Occasionally though, it does spill over, and the gentlemen below have all had their share of fisticuffs both on and off the field.

David Hookes was the saddest case of all, and I couldn't help thinking about this the day I woke up and heard about Jesse Ryder, when he ended up in a coma a couple of years ago. The Australian had all the talent in the world, but went out one night in 2004 in St Kilda, Melbourne, and never came home. He seemed to get into a brawl with nightclub bouncers, one of whom was subsequently cleared of manslaughter, and died after going into cardiac arrest.

His famous comment about bias from the Aussie selectors towards players from New South Wales lives in the memory when he said, 'When they hand out the baggy blue cap of NSW, they also put a baggy green one in a brown paper bag to save them from making two presentations'!

However, it is not all one-way traffic. Shahid Afridi was once asked for his autograph, and proceeded to 'boom-boom' the fan straight in the gob! His Pakistani teammate Inzamam prefers to use the willow, however, wading into the crowd in Canada when some comedian on a megaphone referred to him as 'a potato', replicating the form of Javed Miandad some years earlier, who tried to show Dennis Lillee's head how the hook shot was played after some chat.

Our very own Geoffrey Boycott was convicted in a French court of whacking a lady friend of his in the face. Maybe she questioned his batting average?

Another opening bat, Navjot Singh Sidhu of India, took things a step further when he beat a man to death over a road rage dispute; a conviction which was quashed. Like many a man of such repute, he is now in politics!

Mark Vermeulen was another, and is mentioned elsewhere in this book, as is Monty Panesar, who had a bit of a jostle with his wife in a pub car park until the local constabulary intervened.

Other English cricketers have had their moments too. There must be something about Australia, as apparently Ian Botham didn't like the cut of someone's jib on a flight Down Under and Ian Chappell allegedly did what is known colloquially in a cricket dressing room as a 'Del Shannon' ('Runaway') from Beefy in a hotel car park.

Cricketers at the highest echelons of our game from the modern era are not exempt either. Ricky Ponting 'slipped' in a nightclub back in 1999, giving himself a black eye in the process, and Shiv Chanderpaul once deposited the contents of his revolver into a policeman's hand after mistaking him for a burglar. Hmmm, sounds a familiar defence amongst sportsmen!

I once got booted in a midweek game. We played a side from Essex in a competition which was known in south-east England as the 'Bertie Joel Cup'. Having watched our extremely strong opposition rattle up 350 from their 45 overs, I had gone out to bat at 10–4 and the ball had feathered my thumb second ball. Having stood there and been given not out, I cut the ball for what I thought was definite 3 to the long boundary before being booted up in the air by the irate bowler, having turned for my first run. The matter was swiftly brought to a close by the umpire jumping in, along with their skipper, who did a more than passable impression of Henry Kissinger.

One cricketer from the West Indies wasn't so lucky and that was Leslie Hylton. The opening bowler who played 6 Tests for the Maroon Caps between 1935 and 1939 was convicted of killing his wife and was hanged in 1955. Another West Indian, Roy Gilchrist, also had a bit of a barney with his missus and branded her face with an iron!

Sometimes cricketers are the victims. Percy Hardy of Somerset was found on the floor of a toilet in King's Cross Station in March 1916 with a cut throat – although it was rumoured that he committed suicide, unable to face the traumas of returning to the Somme. Jack Marsh was definitely beaten to death two months later, in what looked like a bad year for cricketers.

Indian first-class player Rajesh Peter was found dead in his flat in 1995 in dubious circumstances, whilst South African Test player Tertius Bosch allegedly died of Guillane-Barré syndrome (whatever that happened to be), although the coroner alluded that he was poisoned, in 2000. Bob Woolmer and Hansie Cronje were others who died in circumstances that the cricketing world has always questioned.

All this goes to show that cricketers are the same as you and me. They have their moments, they have their weaknesses, and no doubt being in the public eye the way they are only adds to the pressure. The stick they receive from crowds for doing their job can only turn up such pressure a few notches. Imagine going to your work, and some bloke behind you tells you that you are crap at your job? I know what I'd do. Yes, they are under huge pressure, but if you are in an office and the receptionist is there all day whilst you are trying to do your desk job to the best of your ability, telling you that you can't do it very well, I am sure that it is the main reason.

I'm sure also, that the gentlemen above won't be the last cricketers to be involved in a punch-up.

SO LONG SWANNY

Graeme Swann retired just before Christmas 2013. With everyone out watching pantomimes during the silly season, the news was sudden and unexpected that Graeme Swann was to retire with immediate effect from all formats of the game. Swann left a couple of cryptic quotes behind on his retirement. Having apologised the week before for describing losing the first 3 Tests in Australia, as being 'arse raped', Swann retired from the pool of Test cricket in dramatic fashion. Here we look back on the career of one of the finest spinners ever to play for England.

Graeme Peter Swann was a prodigious, teenaged talent making his debut for Northamptonshire and was part of the side who won the Under-19 World Cup for England in 1998, along with the likes of Rob Key and Owais Shah. A serious turner of the ball, the off-spinner without a mystery ball was going out of fashion. To chase the dream of England having a world-class spinner in those Muralitharan or Warne-inspired days, it was thought that an 'offie' needed a *doosra*, or even a *teesra*, as they say in India. Everyone needed a wrong 'un in the 1990s, so they said.

Swann rose to the top without this delivery, and in a way was an old-fashioned offie, relying on proper revs making the ball dip at the last minute, thus fooling a batsman in flight.

He wasn't always Mr Popular. Having been picked for the tour of South Africa, following wickets aplenty on the 'Bunsens' at Wantage Road, an oversleeping incident where he missed the bus left him sweating more than a fat lass on a treadmill for his international future. It wasn't just coach Duncan Fletcher that he pissed off with his antics; there were rumours that Darren Gough passed on some of his friendly Barnsley advice as well on that tour, by administering a lethal jab to Swann once.

Having disappeared back to the county game, the likes of Ashley Giles and then county colleague, Monty Panesar, had usurped Swann in the international pecking order. A move to Nottinghamshire beckoned in 2005, before he finally broke his Test virginity in India in dramatic fashion in 2008. Dismissing Gautam Gambhir and Rahul Dravid, Swann was only the second player behind Richard Johnson to take two wickets in their opening over on debut.

Graeme soon picked up his first Test five-fer, and regularly he would pick up a wicket in the first over of a spell. He soon became the scourge of the left-handers, and Swann was someone who utilised the changes in the DRS to his advantage during this era where the power shifted away from the on-pitch umpire. Traditionally left-handers had plonked their foot far enough down the track to off-spinners attacking them from around the wicket, and had been the beneficiaries of the umpire's doubt, but now the camera was found never to lie. Swanny picked up many an lbw via this method.

Swann took the wicket of Mike Hussey to win the Ashes in 2009, and was the main man in South Africa on tour the following winter. In a country where spin bowling has never been a massive success, Ashwell Prince couldn't have been more of Swann's bunny were he to be munching a carrot, and saying 'What's up Doc?'

The defence of the Ashes in 2010–11 was another excellent series for Swann, where he was behind the camera in his excellent *Tour Diaries*, as Swanny made the sprinkler fashionable way before Monty Panesar did on Brighton seafront.

Swann is arguably England's finest ever spin bowler. Jim Laker and Derek Underwood are probably up there in most aficionados' opinions but playing on uncovered wickets was a different scenario. Swann attacked; he wasn't afraid to give it a bit of air, and his chirp and cheekiness made him good value on the interview front. He wasn't an offie who tied people down, firing darts like John Emburey, or even John Lowe for that matter.

However, the Newcastle United fan and musician in Nottingham band Dr Comfort and the Lurid Revelations suddenly retired, no doubt about to spill the beans on lurid revelations in the England camp, and the news to us England fans was definitely not comforting. He left with immediate effect, did not pass go and did not collect his £200. No Kallis or Tendulkar-style *'arriverderci'* for Swanny. He had just suddenly gone.

After England had been spanked in Australia, and amid rumours that he had been dropped, Swann was no more an international cricketer. The timing, it has to be said, was extremely odd. Far be it from me to tell international players when to retire, a swansong (pardon the pun) in front of 91,000 people at the MCG or the SCG shouldn't be turned down by anyone at any stage. I can't imagine a footballer retiring after the World Cup group games or a British Lion just going off home halfway through a tour.

Piers Morgan, in an explosive interview with us in March 2014, described Swann as a 'gutless egotist'. To represent your country is something to be proud of, and Swann was one of the proudest. Whether he couldn't take it anymore, like Trott, who knows? All does not seem happy in the England camp, and the trip to Australia in 2013–14 will go down as one of the most torrid in English history.

Swann left obviously having a dig at someone. Some blame KP, which Swann was quick to deny, some blame Broad. Others blame the Aussies, but maybe he had just had enough? The truth will come out in a book or press release one day, I'm sure.

A media career no doubt beckons for him, but we should be proud that we have witnessed a fine career. A total of 255 Test wickets in 60 games, some useful contributions with the bat, averaging 22, and a fine second slip pouching many a decent chance, are top stats. I will always remember him as good fun to watch. He attacked, he looped it and wasn't afraid to get hit. Part of the England team who rose to No. 1 in the world, he also achieved No 2 personally. He was one of the best English spinners ever.

It's just a shame he retired when and how he did. His career deserved a better send-off.

PAUL SMITH – THE ROCK AND ROLLER OF CRICKET

Paul Smith was a man well known to anyone who followed the domestic scene back in the 1980s. Not to be confused with the fashionista, *this* Paul Smith was a scenester in his own right. With long flowing hair, he was a reasonably brisk bowler and could also bat, preferring to give it a thump at the top of the order. When I said the above to ESPN Cricinfo journalist George Dobell, he exclaimed, 'he wasn't reasonably brisk. He was quick as fuck. Bob Willis described him as the quickest white man in the world, and even Allan Donald said he could be quicker than him.' A member of the famous Warwickshire treble-winning team of 1994 under Bob Woolmer and Brian Lara, Smith's life started to unravel a few years later as he descended into a pit of despair; the drugs were no longer recreational and took over his life.

Smith was a decent player without being a brilliant one. Born in Newcastle in 1964, he scored 1,500 runs aged just 22 for the

Bears, who he had joined when he was 19 years old. He finished up with two hat-tricks, and played in six One Day finals at Lord's, in one of which he was named as 'Man of the Match'. He was part of the team that did the unprecedented Treble in 1994, and he won the Double in 1995. There have been far better players that have won far less silverware in the game.

The Warwickshire team of the 1990s, as well as being hugely successful on the pitch, seemed to have a drug connection, with Dermot Reeve and a few others who seemed to have a penchant for the white line, and I'm not just talking about the boundary at Edgbaston. More Bogota, less Birmingham, shall we say? Smith was an integral part of that dressing room, along with his good friend, wicketkeeper Keith Piper, and both were integral to the success on the pitch, yet ultimate failure off it. Piper was another who had his career terminated for using cannabis.

Smith admits he was out of control. Dermot Reeve described him as 'cricket's first bimbo', in reference to his long, blond mane and his party lifestyle. Stories of him having sex on aeroplanes on pre-season tours to South Africa, much to the chagrin of the late Bob Woolmer, or going out to bat completely pissed against Malcolm Marshall at Bournemouth, were rife and it was only a matter of time before he got caught.

The Hampshire bowler said, 'Don't worry Smithy, this won't take long', and a few balls later the Warwickshire player was on his way back, albeit having taken a few steps in a different direction to the pavilion, before being shown the way by a kind Hampshire fielder. He implies that he wasn't the only player using recreational drugs at the time, and many high-profile internationals were too. In fact, Smith was offered £90,000 by a Fleet Street red top to dish the dirt on other players with whom he had consumed narcotics. Despite being on his last legs financially, Smith refused to take the money. The problem with Paul Smith though, is that the drugs weren't just recreational, they were part of his daily diet.

In 1997, Smith was banned by the ECB for admitting to using a cocktail of cocaine, speed and cannabis. At the same time, Paul Merson admitted a similar thing in the world of football. Whilst one Paul had a lot of help and support from his club Arsenal and the Professional Footballers' Association, Paul Smith got a two-year ban which finished his career. He then went out to South Africa, and the unconventional Smith became the first white player to play for St Augustine's, a township club in Cape Town that counts the brilliant Basil D'Oliveira as one of their alumni. He didn't do things by the book.

It was after this that Smith started to struggle with life, and he moved out to Los Angeles in the United States. His marriage had broken up, his best friend Keith Piper having had an affair with his wife for a number of years, and his visitation rights to his children were sporadic to say the least.

The conventional amongst us would associate Compton and cricket with Dennis, Nick or Leslie, but for the idiosyncratic Smith, the suburb of Compton, which was better known for gang killing between the 'Bloods' and the 'Crips', became home. At one point during this period of his life Smith didn't even have a home and would often sleep rough. The world of Warwickshire County Cricket Club and being a professional sportsman seemed a million miles away as he became penniless.

It was during this sad period, when there were days when he often went without food, that he began the shoots of recovery

which started to turn his life around. Smith started to coach the local kids there and, despite some sad stories such as being desperate for money to bury one of his players who had hit the crystal meth once too often, he was doing some great work in a deprived community. He would use his experiences playing cricket to help children stay clear of gun crime, and there is no doubt that he has saved many lives.

It was here that he set up a charity which has blossomed and burgeoned over the years and now does some fantastic work helping children with HIV throughout Africa. The roots were formed by Smith giving under-privileged children the chance in Compton, and he was awarded a 'Certificate of Appreciation' by the city of Los Angeles in 2003 for helping to turn youngsters away from a life of crime. He also works with the Prince's Trust.

Paul Smith is now clean, and away from the excessive past that nearly ruined him. His life can still be chaotic, but he often gives interviews citing the fact that players in his day were not given the support for an illness. The decision to just ban him when other sports gave such support is strange, and thank God cricket has moved on. The game throws up lots of interesting characters and the game is richer for having had Paul Smith as part of its furniture over the years. There are many amusing tales regarding Paul Smith. Buying the suit that the Proclaimers wore in one of their videos for £1,000 is one.

Characters like him don't come around too often and should be treasured.

BROTHERS IN ARMS

Think of cricketing brothers, and you look back at W.G. and E.M. Grace for England, or the famous Walker brothers at Middlesex, who gave their well-known ground to where I now play my club cricket in Southgate, north London. During the same era, you had the Bannerman or Gregory brothers for Australia. Then, moving on, you had the Bedsers followed by the Comptons, Dennis and Leslie, in the mid-twentieth century.

The 1960s gave us the Mohammads for Pakistan, four of them to be precise, and the 1970s gave us the Chappells and the Greigs. The 1980s threw up the Crowes, whilst the 1990s offered us probably the best pair ever to play Test cricket in the famous Waugh twins. Throw in the Flowers, the Hollioakes and the Akmals, and there are many famous brothers who have played cricket over the years.

However, the two I want to put in this book are characters of the game who have made me laugh on numerous occasions, and I have had the privilege of interviewing them both over the last year. Ladies and gentlemen, I bring you the Shantrys ...

Brian Shantry was a county cricketer who played for Gloucestershire at the end of the 1970s before the birth of his son Adam in 1982, followed by Jack in 1988. Not only did he pass on his love for cricket to them both, but also his love for Bristol City, although Adam tells me that this passion nearly spilled over into violence after a Bristol derby, thanks to Brian passing on the benefit of his wit to those fans from the other side of the city. Having given them short shrift, and soaking them with water, only a bit of quick thinking got them out of trouble. Skinhead supporters of their rivals, Bristol Rovers, came close to smashing up a Warwickshire-sponsored car stuck in heavy traffic, before a sharp U-turn into an oncoming carriageway got them out of trouble. God knows what Adam's employers at Edgbaston would have thought, but thanks to his sharp driving skills it was less 'Amiss', more 'near miss'.

Apart from teaching them about all things Ashton Gate, Brian also taught them to swim once by throwing them into a local canal with armbands on and shouting 'Watch out for the barges', leading them both to ask questions about their father's parsimony in later life – when a man tries to save £2.50 by chucking his kids into a Weil's disease-ridden waterway, instead of using the local lido, you'd tend to agree with the boys. Talking of swimming, I had the privilege of chatting with Adam before he crossed the Channel last year in aid of the Tom Maynard Trust. Brian's tough love must have worked after all.

Adam had a career that took him to Northamptonshire, Warwickshire and then Glamorgan, before retiring with knee injuries in 2011. Jack still plies his trade at Worcestershire, where he has been for a number of years, and even scored a match-winning hundred towards the end of 2014 to help guarantee them promotion. Their love of Bristol City has also been transferred on to the cricket pitch, with Jack informing us that he tried sledging fellow Red, Marcus Trescothick, with songs of their beloved Robins, singing tunes such as 'Drink up thee zider', although whether it worked or not is a moot point as the Somerset left-hander got a double hundred.

Adam, whilst at Glamorgan, had learned a differing form of sledging, having been enlightened to the following off-putting tip from one current professional. He told me:

When standing close to the batsman, remove your penis from your trousers while he isn't looking, and dangle it in front of you. As the bowler is reaching the end of his mark, and with your penis entering the batsman's field of vision, ask him if he wants to see his mum's lipstick.

Saying that, Adam wasn't so happy when, having given West Indian quick Tino Best a send-off, the God-fearing paceman responded with 'Let's see how much chat you have when you bat. Cocksucker'.

Both also inherited their father's left-arm swing bowling, and both are useful batsmen too. Jack tells me that being a southpaw is a useful way of scratching up the pitch, although often he had to distract umpires such as David Millns by pointing out a pretty woman in the crowd. When his attention was elsewhere, Jack would scratch away until his heart was content so the spinners in his side would be able to bowl into the rough.

Jack has an action that could only be described as idiosyncratic, and Adam tells me that this is because he batted all the time when they were kids in the garden. When it was his turn to bowl, Jack would often disappear indoors to watch television and Adam tells us that Jack has been punished for his laziness in later life by being given a ridiculous action.

Both Shantry brothers are obviously popular with their teammates. At the heart of the banter that bonds all good sides together, the dressing room and the humour that goes with it is hugely important to them. Whether it is Jack christening a teammate 'Bruce Forsyth', after said colleague told him that his chances were looking good with a member of the opposite sex should he 'play his cards right', or another player's conquest of a reality TV star and how she got the ball to reverse swing the following day (something that couldn't possibly be repeated in such a classy publication such as this), they have stories a plenty.

Adam, meanwhile, shared a changing room with Tom Maynard, leading him to swim in his memory. Loyalty is obviously high up on both brothers' agenda.

One thing that always amuses every cricketer at levels, whether you play for your fourth eleven or for your country, is the reaction of teammates when out for a low score, or if given a shocker of a decision from an umpire. Adam recalls Paul Coverdale breaking his hand on a dressing room wall, leading to a summer sabbatical of five weeks, whilst Jack tells us about Vikram Solanki kicking a wall and getting his foot stuck in it, still resplendent in his batting pads.

There may be other brothers who will grace the record books, and others who will make more of a mark on the pitch, but off the pitch these two have given me plenty of good laughs and anecdotes from their careers and therefore they deserve their place in this book. I can only imagine what Christmas dinner is like round at chez Shantry. Cricket needs characters like these, and long may it continue to produce them.

THE FAB FOUR

In September 2013 the news coming out of the north-east was that Steve Harmison was retiring from all forms of cricket, hot on the tails of Matthew Hoggard. In the same month that we heard the announcement that Simon Jones is only going to be playing T20 cricket, and along with the long-retired Andrew Flintoff, we look back on these four outstanding pace bowlers who, between 2004 and 2005, were arguably the best attack in the world.

I loved this fab four in their own special way; each of them had their good and bad points, yet you can imagine they'd have been a good laugh to go for a beer with, as well as being a fine quartet of seam bowlers, causing problems for the best in the world.

Let's start with 'Hoggy'. The man born in Pudsey played for his home county of Yorkshire for thirteen years, and was the 'shop floor man' of the England bowling attack, according to Michael Vaughan. If Hoggy bowled a jaffa, Vaughan would get him back to his mark quickly, telling him to bowl line and length and not to try too much. A bowler of conventional swing, he would boomerang it about, and after some outstanding performances for his county, the Yorkshireman made his England debut in 2000.

It was in 2004, though, that the man from the White Rose County really blossomed, and a hat-trick in Barbados gave

England their first series win in the Windies since 1969. A cheeky 12 wickets followed in the Cape Town Test, and he had become an excellent exponent of the art of swinging. It was no surprise that he became a wonderful foil to the pace and aggression of Steve Harmison.

My favourite Hoggy moment, though, is not his wonderful cover drive off Brett Lee, his field to Hayden or nipping one back into Justin Langer's pads. No, it is Matthew Hoggard who was rumoured to have been the guilty man who watered Tony Blair's plants in the garden of No. 10 that infamous time! Still, at least it wasn't on the victory tour bus, like Jason Leonard, who was caught short in 2003. Apparently the English prop relieved himself in a champagne bottle and, unaware that the bus was about to brake suddenly in heavy London traffic, spilt some down the chinos of a nearby Lewis Moody, causing the Queen's corgis to take an extra special interest in the Leicester flanker a few hours later.

Hoggy, a man of principle, moved on to Leicestershire, and led them to T20 success in the 2011 final, remembered for an outstanding catch by Paul Nixon.

Simon Jones was the opposite of Hoggard. The son of ex-England International Jeff Jones, the man from West Wales played his club cricket at Dafen CC, a ground where The Middle Stump's Liam has been known to occasionally get given out, lbw.

Bursting on to the England scene aged just 23, it was as a batsman that he caught the eye on his debut versus India with a sparkling 44. A decent bowler, who could get it above 90mph on a regular basis, he was taken to Australia before suffering an injury that still makes me sick when I see it on YouTube. Sliding to field on a sand-filled surface, Jones sticks in the ground and his body goes over the top, snapping his anterior cruciate ligament as easily as Matthew Hayden's temper when Jones threw a ball at him a few years later in a One Day International (I loved Jones for winding Hayden up, and you could see we really had the Aussies rattled).

Jones battled back and got himself fit for the 2005 Ashes, and reverse swinging the ball at his pace certainly caused the Australians problems. One of my favourite sights ever in Ashes history was Michael Clarke leaving a ball that reversed and took his off pole out of the earth. Every good, English, teenaged, up-and-coming quick bowler should fantasise over such an orgasmic delivery. He was unplayable that day at Old Trafford and, reversing it at his pace, it was no surprise.

Jones could, and should, have been the best of this bunch, but injuries curtailed his appearances. Despite a couple of moves to Worcestershire and Hampshire, Jones finished his career with his beloved Glamorgan in a One Day final at Lord's, and bowled beautifully in a losing attempt to win the YB40.

Steven Harmison was all about bounce, and was the stuff of nightmares when he got it in the right place. No less a great judge of being an opening bat than Michael Atherton once referred to 'pace not being a problem with bowlers as they are all quick anyway, but bounce is'. As a man dismissed regularly by Glenn McGrath and Curtly Ambrose, he should know!

A lifelong Newcastle United fan, 'Harmy' replaced Jones for his debut in 2003, and was spearheading the England attack a year later.

I will never, ever forget that 7–12 in Jamaica as we bowled the Windies out for 47. I will never, ever forget the umbrella field that was set that day, not seen since the days of the Windies quicks in the 1980s. I will never, ever forget him cutting Ricky Ponting's cheek at Lord's as we sent out a message to the Aussies that we meant serious business in that summer of 2005, and I will never, ever forget the slower ball that foxed Michael Clarke. However, the wicket that never was is the one that will stick with all Englishmen forever, with Kasprowicz fending one off of his chin and gloving it to Geraint Jones as England won at Edgbaston by 2 runs, even though technically it shouldn't have counted as Kaspa was not holding the bat at the time. If we had lost that one, we'd never have recovered.

Harmison was seriously quick and a real handful. He would get bounce from nowhere and, when delivered at 90mph plus, batsmen didn't seem to fancy it. He went through Pakistan a year later in a similar way to how Pakistani cuisine went through your average England player's guts a few years earlier – quickly, and causing a few brown stains on the back of your whites. He could also bat a bit, and would often give it a slap lower down the order, but he picked up some excellent wickets for England and worried and hurried the very best batsmen in the world.

He was big mates with Andrew Flintoff and 'Freddie' was a serious cricketer, fielder and drinker. The Lancastrian made his debut for England against South Africa at Trent Bridge in 1998, in that famous Donald/Atherton stare-out, and then took Surrey for a blistering 135 in a televised quarter-final of the NatWest Trophy. After receiving criticism for his weight during his younger years, he told Paul Allott in a post-match interview after receiving the 'Man of the Match' award that it 'wasn't bad for a fat lad'.

By 2005, Flintoff was outstanding with both bat and ball. He had ankle problems, but got himself fit and the over he bowled at Justin Langer and Ricky Ponting at Edgbaston is worth watching over and over. A hundred at Trent Bridge, along with serious bursts of pace; he was not only 'Man of the Series', but ICC Player of the Year, Sports Personality of the Year and joined Tom Finney as a freeman of his home town of Preston. England loved Freddie, as he was the sort of bloke you could imagine having a pint with.

My favourite story of his, though, has to be the 'cocktail' he unwittingly stirred for teammate Gary Yates, with the operative syllable being 'cock'. Freddie iced his manhood under the instruction of David Lloyd, after being hit in the box whilst having a net on a hot day. He put his glass full of ice down on the table in the dressing room afterwards, before a parched Yates walked in five minutes later and proceeded to down the cold water in one!

In a way, I am sad that we won't ever see these guys grace a cricket pitch again, and in another way I am grateful and privileged that I saw them together for England at their prime. They were a real handful, like hyenas hunting in packs, and for that you have to salute this brilliant, wonderful fab four. Not only fine cricketers, but also fine characters of the game.

Thanks for the memories.

IRON MIKE ATHERTON

As England start to struggle again, a man who was wheeled out in press conferences regularly in the 1990s should know how the current England skipper feels. Now one of the finest journalists around, Michael Atherton was a decent player, and tried his best in a time when it wasn't always easy for English cricket.

Athers was a hard-nosed, obdurate, opening bat, dubbed the 'cockroach' by Steve Waugh because he was hard to stamp out, and the man who relied on timing when he played has since become a hard-hitting journalist and pundit.

Athers was born in Manchester in 1968, and was a schoolboy prodigy. He scored runs aplenty at Manchester Grammar School, where he broke numerous records. Incidentally, many of these were broken by John Crawley a few years later, but with 'Iron Mike' this led to captaining the England Under-19 team at the age of just 16.

As well as his batting, he was a promising leg spinner – taking 6 wickets against the MCC – and he was the darling of the North.

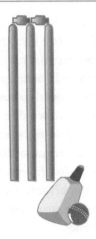

He then went to Cambridge University where he batted regularly with another fine journalist, the *Sunday Telegraph*'s Steve James. This team were good enough to reach the quarter-finals of the Benson & Hedges Cup as combined universities, virtually unheard of for this team who were whipped more times in the 1980s than Frank Bough.

In his autobiography *Opening Up*, Athers claims that his nickname of 'FEC', which stood for 'Future England Captain', was changed slightly by his county colleagues to become 'Fucking Educated C***'!

He had already scored hundreds for Lancashire at this stage, and in 1989 Athers was selected against Australia for England in the fifth Test. He was fortunate enough to miss the bombardment and the injuries sustained on the winter tour to the Windies in 1990 under Graham Gooch, instead getting a trip on the A tour to Zimbabwe.

The following summer, he made his mark on his return to the full side. Hundreds against India and New Zealand came, and faced with an even sterner test in Australia, he batted well, scoring an excellent hundred in Sydney. A touch player, he was a decent hooker and puller too, and the hands of cover point would always be warm with Athers at the crease.

When the Aussies arrived in 1993, Athers scored a fine 99 at Lord's before being comically, or tragically, run out going for a third. After Graham Gooch had had enough of the captaincy later that summer, his fellow opening partner was made England captain. He even won his second game in charge against Australia at the Oval, the first time England had beaten the Aussies in 18 Tests.

A losing tour to the Windies followed, before the home series against South Africa which was famous for the 'dirt in the pocket'. Athers was caught on TV drying one side of the ball by rubbing dirt on it, and when asked by the match referee if he had anything, he responded in the negative. This was clearly untrue, although bowlers regularly dried their hands on the dirt and soil on the crease. He didn't actually do anything wrong to be honest, apart from not be completely truthful with Peter Burge, and Illy fined him a couple of grand for his trouble. The tabloid press had a field day, but Athers shut them up with 99 (again!) in his next knock.

Many of his finest knocks were when he was 'up against it'. His marathon 185 not out to save the Test in Johannesburg, on a quick one with Allan Donald steaming in at him, was one of the finest knocks by an Englishmen in Test history.

After resigning the captaincy, I am sure everyone will remember him nicking off to the aforementioned Donald at Trent Bridge a few years later, and being given not out, much to the ire of the blond South African. This was Test cricket at its most compelling. Athers always liked to stare out the bowlers, believing they had to return to their mark sooner or later, whilst a batsman could just stand there.

He eventually retired in 2001, due to the cocktail of painkillers he would have to take just to get his back through a match. The stats don't quite tell the story behind a fine batsman. On the negative side, no batsman has scored 6,000 Test runs with such a low average, but he also had to face a barrage of some of the finest bowlers ever to play the game. Glenn McGrath dismissed him nineteen times, whilst Curtly and Courtney dismissed him seventeen times each. He also shares the dubious distinction, alongside Steve Harmison, of the most ducks for England.

Since retirement, he has worked for Channel 4 and then Sky dealing with commentary, whilst writing a fine column in *The Times*. A dry, humorous journo, he isn't frightened to tackle some tough subjects, such as questioning the One Day credentials of Alastair Cook, leading to a drunken rant from fellow Lancastrian, Andrew Flintoff.

He is a man who has always liked to do things differently – marrying a South American wife, for instance – and has been mentioned by numerous people as one of the scruffiest individuals ever to have stepped on to a cricket pitch. Think of the rough side of a ball when a side are trying to get it to reverse swing, and you have Atherton's apparel, according to those close to him. The contrast between his kit bag, and the immaculate kit of his opening partner Alec Stewart (the smooth side of the ball), had to be seen to be believed apparently.

Athers will go down in history as a man who tried his best. A man who led the line, and led from the front during a time when English cricket was at a low ebb. If we could have seen Athers at a time of central contracts, the stats may tell a different story. A great thinker of the game, we are lucky we now have him in the commentary box, and his insightful comments add value to not only Sky's team, but make him one of the finest journalists around.

MONTY MANIA

Mudhsuden Singh Panesar was born in Luton in April 1982, and has become one of the most recognisable English cricketers of recent years. I first heard of him in around 1999, when speaking with the Bedfordshire Cricket Development Officer, David Mercer, over many beers as my club had just beaten his side, Dunstable Town, in a league match. Dave explained that they had a young left-arm spinner who would go all the way and he was world-class. Monty was then named as one of the sportsmen to watch in the millennium, and was in the national press.

It all started for him at his hometown club, Luton Town & Indians, and under the guidance of Hitu Naik, now a respected umpire on the Hertfordshire league circuit. Monty was a left-arm seamer, but massive fingers meant that he was asked to bowl spin, and he was not only accurate but also turned it miles.

After completing his studies at Bedford School, having transferred from a comprehensive in Luton once his cricket made people sit up and take notice, he had the choice between Essex and Northamptonshire. Both had left-arm spinners in John Childs or Nick Cook trying to tempt him, and Monty was a man in demand. He chose the latter, and his performances on the Bunsen burners at Wantage Road in tandem with Graeme Swann were something that would be seen on the international stage a few years later.

Wickets arrived, and most importantly, so did control. Miserly Monty didn't go for many runs, and he was christened 'The Prince of Parsimony'. The international stage beckoned, and he was picked on the tour to India. Being a Sikh on the opposing side to most Indians made him massive news in this cricket-mad country, and having been picked for the first Test alongside Alastair Cook, Monty's first wicket in Test cricket was none other than Sachin Tendulkar. Sachin gave him a signed ball after the game with the words 'Never Again' written on it in reference to getting trapped lbw, but Monty did trap him the next year in exactly the same fashion.

On this tour to India, Monty sought out another slow left-armer who had played at Northamptonshire in Bishen Bedi. With a similar action, the patka-wearing Panesar has regularly been compared with the turban-wearing Bedi. Monty has a smooth action, fairly mechanical, and accuracy was his biggest strength.

It was also on this tour that we found out something else about Monty. His bowling may have been world-class, but his fielding was still club standard. In his first Test he dropped a sitter when MS Dhoni picked him out at long off, before the Indian keeper let him have another go just three balls later, which he held.

He became a cult hero back at home. People would go to the matches wearing a Monty patka and beard. Kids loved him, and he became a legend to many Asian youngsters both in the UK and in India. However, it wasn't long before his career then started to go downhill. Although he was still picking up wickets in the county game, appearances for England became more sporadic, and Graeme Swann overtook him as the frontline spinner. The critiques said he was too mechanical, scared to toss it up and give the ball air, and that his bowling was too much of the same. He would be picked for tours, but often appearing irregularly. Saying that, on his return to India in 2012–13 when England won, he out-bowled Swann during that victorious series.

He moved to Sussex, and it was here that things started to go seriously downhill. Rumours of drinking astonished cricket fans who knew him as teetotal, and the police were called to an incident in a pub car park where he had an altercation with his wife.

It was in the summer of 2013, though, that he really astonished the cricketing cognoscenti. Having been recently separated, Monty had gone seriously 'off the rails', as they say in dressing room terminology, and he was arrested in Brighton after a night on the sauce. For those of you unfamiliar with the seaside town, there are a number of bars and nightclubs under the arches of the promenade, which you need to go down to from street level to reach the beach. Monty, having been ejected from a nightclub at 4 a.m. for hassling women, decided to wreak his revenge on the bouncers by urinating on them from the street above. Chased by the fleeing mob, he sought refuge in a fast food restaurant before the police arrived to save him. YouTube footage shows Panesar crying for help, and he looked to be relieved to be arrested for relieving himself.

There were many jokes flying around, with Monty being referred to as Sacha Distel (presumably 'Raindrops Keep Falling on My Head') and many other gags which amused the twitterati, but not everyone knew the full story. This was an international sportsman arrested for pissing on someone, and as you can imagine, the tabloid press had a field day. Monty was sacked by Sussex, and went to Essex in a move that wasn't deemed the most supportive amongst those in the know.

With England crying out for a spinner after Graeme Swann's retirement, this should be Monty's time. However, his move to Essex hasn't been a huge success as I write this, and he has also been dropped twice; once on disciplinary charges for missing a team meeting and once because of poor form.

Cricket needs characters like Monty Panesar, though, and he is a role model for young Asian kids coming through which will only improve English cricket. He has given a lot to the game, and I can only wish him well in his battles on and off the pitch.

ALVIDA SACHIN

Sachin Tendulkar retired in November 2013, and he will surely go down as one of the greats of the game. Fittingly, he retired at Mumbai's famous Wankhede Stadium, where it all started for him four decades previously. The use of the word 'great' has become way too prevalent in these days of social networking, but he really does belong in that category and will go down as one of the best batsmen of all time. Some say Bradman, some say Tendulkar for the title; both were similar in stature.

Here, we have a look at the career of the 'Little Master from Mumbai' and come to the conclusion that we may have just witnessed the career of the best player ever.

He came to light in my cricketing brain when, as a 16 year old, he made his debut against Pakistan. I was lucky enough to see him a few months later at Lord's, in 1990, in a match famous for a relentless 333 not out, by Graham Gooch. It was also a game in which I lost a fiver, which can be read about in the chapter on Eddie Hemmings.

Tendulkar then had a stint at Yorkshire, becoming their first overseas pro in 1992, before joining a young line-up, along with Dravid and Ganguly, that had Indian fans as excited as Jonathan Ross or Roy Hodgson when asked what the currency is in India. Yorkshiremen jest that they made him the player that he was, but in reality, although he had a decent campaign, he wasn't a superstar there by any stretch of the imagination.

The 5ft 5in Tendulkar was part of a formidable Indian middle order with Rahul Dravid and Sourav Ganguly, and carried the weight of a nation on his shoulders every time he went out to bat. In a country of 1.3 billion people, he coped with becoming one of the sport's superstars admirably, and he became a global brand.

He smashed statistic after statistic, and barely a year went by in recent years where he didn't reach one milestone or another. Record after record has been broken by him: 34,000 international runs – that is serious going. Chuck in 200 Tests, and the first man to a hundred centuries, and we can see why Sachin amassed a staggering 662 matches in international cricket. It's just phenomenal.

Have a look at how good the statistics are of Michael Clarke or Alastair Cook after 100 Test matches. Add them together and that is virtually what you get with Sachin. Amazingly, there was a stat in December 2013 where both of them had exactly half of Sachin's career stats. Sachin had played 200 Test matches, when they were both playing in their one hundredth. Cook had scored 7,955 Test runs, and Clarke 7,966, which adds up to exactly the 15,921 of Tendulkar. Throw in the combined 51 Test centuries that they had scored, which again is exactly the amount the Little Master finished with and this was a truly amazing stat. Cook and Clarke are both fine batsmen in their own right, so it goes to show how good Sachin was. Such longevity of high-class batsmanship defines him, and to have him in your side – as India did – would be the equivalent of having both Clarke *and* Cook in your team.

His bowling wasn't bad either. Bowling offies, leggies, or a bit of seam up depending on his mood, he could be a tidy bowler and a breaker of partnerships. What I will always remember him for, though, was his textbook straight drive. Like Bradman, a small and compact player, in a similar way to another quality bat from Mumbai in Sunil Gavaskar, with amazing concentration allied with Indian wristiness, he just churned out the runs year after year, over a twenty-four-year Test career. I'm not going to name all of the records that he broke as they are way too long to be listed, and I am too lazy a writer to research them, as they will take me forever!

He also earned some serious wonga. 'Pwoper dough', as Danny Dyer, or the aforementioned Hodgson or Ross would say.

The fifty-first richest sportsman in the world earned a mere $22 million in 2012 alone. He became bigger than a film star in India, bigger than David Beckham in the UK, and on a par with the likes of Brad Pitt and Tom Cruise for celebrity status. The weight of pressure must have been immense, and he admitted to often driving around Mumbai at night because of the mass adulation he received everywhere he went. To cope with the pressures with such longevity is astonishing.

It is amazing that he rarely snapped under the constant spotlight, and the only two real bits of controversy in his career were a spat with referee Mike Denness over ball-tampering in South Africa in 2001, followed a year later by a ruckus with the Indian finance minister about him paying tax on the importation of a Ferrari.

Matthew Hayden, on tour in India in 1998, allegedly said: 'I have seen God and he bats No. 4 for India'. He wasn't wrong, although Sachin himself said, 'I am not a god of cricket. I make mistakes, God doesn't.'

He played such a big part in Indian cricket as they became a superpower on the world stage, and cricket fans worldwide, not just his adoring legions in India, will miss the man that has been a mainstay in the middle order for what seems like an eternity. With a career that has mirrored the growth in India's economy, in the later years of his career and the advent of the IPL, Sachin's career can be twinned with India's rise as serious force in world cricket.

With millions in the bank from a sporting career alone, along with a chain of restaurants and a healthcare and fitness product empire, amongst other business interests, he never needs to work again. Maybe a move to politics for this fine ambassador for the game?

Whatever he does, this legendary, record-breaking cricketer will go down as one of the greats of all time, if not the best ever. His runs were amassed in a different era from Bradman –

I personally don't want to compare players from differing eras like that. Let's just enjoy them for what they are, and the joy they have brought to so many cricket fans around the world.

Saying that, this English cricket fan was always glad to see the back of Tendulkar when we played India, as no doubt my grandparents' generation were when Bradman was back in the hutch.

Whoever you think was the best player of all time can be debated all night over a pint in your cricket club bar, and we may have just witnessed the curtain call on the career of the best yet. Who knows? Whatever the outcome, all cricketing fans of the modern era can only say, 'Alvida Sachin'.

NAUGHTY NASSER

The Sky commentary box contained five former England cricket captains in 2013. Nasser Hussain was arguably England's most successful skipper out of the five, although he was booed at the end of his first series as England hit bottom of the world rankings in 1999 after losing to New Zealand. A harsh man at times, Nasser cajoled, bullied and shaped England back into a decent outfit and, although wasn't overly popular with some of his man-management techniques, deserves a hell of a lot of credit along with Duncan Fletcher for turning around England's fortunes.

Nasser was born in Madras, India, in 1968 to father, Joe, who had played for Tamil Nadu in India. The Hussain family settled in Ilford on the borders of east London and Essex in 1975. Joe ran the indoor cricket school there, and a young Nasser was an aspiring leg spin bowler, once claiming the castle of none other than Essex legend, Graham Gooch.

I first heard about him and the family in the mid-1980s. Our Sunday side used to play Fives & Heronians, and Nasser's brother, Mel, would regularly improve his batting average against us!

Mel played for Worcestershire for a bit, and another brother, Abbas, also played Essex second-eleven cricket.

The other time I had heard the Hussain name mentioned was through a bloke I knew who was representing South of England schools, and who played for Southgate Cricket Club at the time. My mate was down to be twelfth man when skipper Hussain ran into a sightscreen, turning it various shades of red and white whilst doing pre-match fielding drills, and the 'twelfthers' got to play after all!

A schoolboy prodigy, he played for England Schools with the 'golden boy of the north' Mike Atherton, and the likes of Martin Bicknell and Mark Ramprakash, before he joined Essex in 1987 whilst still playing for Durham University. England came calling, with a baptism of fire in the West Indies on the 1990 tour skippered by mentor, Graham Gooch.

He was then discarded for a while for being too hot-headed, and returned in 1993 only to be dropped again and not picked for a full six years after his debut. It was this series against India, with England having tried all sorts, such as Jason Gallian at No. 3, which was the start of a proper run in the Test team. Hussain scored a couple of tons and was named 'Man of the Series'.

He became skipper after the departure of Alec Stewart, for the series against New Zealand in 1999. Hussain was booed mercilessly at the last game at the Oval, and was subject to the wrath of the tabloid press as England hit the bottom of the Test rankings. It was then that Duncan Fletcher came on board, and although Fletcher and Hussain had never even previously met, between them they started to turn the fortunes of English cricket around. It was here that the foundations for the 2005 Ashes series were put in place.

Under these two, England became harder to beat, and they would weave intricate plans on how to deal with the opposition. It was quite possibly the most successful blind date in history.

Hussain was an imaginative skipper with his field placings and tactics, and his part in the process of England's rejuvenation as a successful Test-playing nation should never be underestimated. The mental hardness of both of them rubbed off on the side, with Fletcher's South African toughness, combined with the Essex streetwise mentality of Hussain, who had been schooled in a strict Indian upbringing.

There were some downsides to him, though. A temper, always just simmering under the surface, erupted once as he trashed a team fridge after a dubious lbw decision in Pakistan, and rumours of the way he spoke to players, scorers and even dressing room attendants at times do not cover him in glory. According to some, Hussain, even to this day, is an appalling loser on the golf course!

Nasser famously pointed to his back after scoring a ton at Lord's to the No. 3 shirt, after copping some stick from the press box, and in the match after he relinquished the captaincy he was supposed to have told Graeme Smith, 'Who the fuck do you think you are?'

Hussain maximised what he had, got the most out of his talent and played on the edge. Even his big mate Graham Thorpe didn't escape the wrath of the Hussain tongue when he was England skipper, with him threatening to send Thorpe home after the Surrey left-hander was moping around during his matrimonial difficulties.

I was privileged to watch his last game, and fittingly he hit the winning runs for his hundred as England beat New Zealand at Lord's. A hundred on debut from Andrew Strauss persuaded Hussain there was new blood coming through so, selflessly retiring, he ended up with 96 Test caps, 45 of them as skipper.

He ended up with over 30,000 runs in all forms of cricket and with 52 hundreds. A technique that wasn't perfect, with a tendency to open the face and run the ball down to third man, was tightened up in later years, and the ability to change, think on his feet and in a way be streetwise, is what epitomises

Hussain's career. He got the most out of his limited England team as well, and for that reason he should go down as one of the finest leaders in the modern era.

A move to the commentary box to sit alongside those who had pointed out that he wasn't a One Day No. 3 happened in 2004, and he provides insightful knowledge on the game. A thoughtful commentator, he isn't afraid to let rip when he needs to, and he had a bit of a 'barney' as they say in east London, with Ravi Shastri over India's reluctance to bring in the DRS a couple of years ago.

Controversial, just like he was as a player, he makes a decent commentator.

ARISE SIR IAN ...

David Brent, on Ian Botham:

> People see me, and they see the suit, and they go: 'you're not fooling anyone', they know I'm rock and roll through and through. But you know that old thing, live fast, die young? Not my way. Live fast, sure, live too bloody fast sometimes, but die young? Die old. That's the way – not orthodox, I don't live by 'the rules' you know. And if there's one other person who's influenced me in that way I think, someone who is a maverick, someone who does that to the system, then, it's Ian Botham. Because Beefy will happily say 'that's what I think of your selection policy, yes I've hit the odd copper, yes I've enjoyed the old dooby, but will you piss off and leave me alone, I'm walking to John O'Groats for some mongs'.

Having played Australia in 2013 home and away in an Ashes double, there was the odd mention of a chap called Ian Botham over the year. What he did, on a cricket ground in Leeds, in Birmingham and in Manchester, back in that riot-torn summer of 1981, may have got the odd comment still thirty-two years later. When you think back to that era, you think of Charles and Diana, and Britain in pieces as the inner cities exploded, but if one person defines that summer for me as a kid, it has to be Sir Ian Botham.

Ian Terence Botham was born in 1955 in Heswall, on the Wirral in Cheshire, also the birthplace of Jim Bowen, Andy McCluskey from OMD and the brilliant John Peel. He soon moved to Yeovil in the West Country, and at 18 made his debut for Somerset. He came to national recognition in a televised game in 1974 when the quick West Indian, Andy Roberts, smashed him in the mouth. Beefy simply gobbed out a couple of teeth, spat the odd bit of blood out and continued his innings. In later years he would have downed anything to do with claret, let alone spit it out.

At this time Botham was a flatmate of the West Indian Vivian Richards, and the lifelong friends were later knighted. Over the winter 'Both' had a spell in grade cricket in Australia which was a tough learning curve, and it was here that his tête-à-tête with Ian Chappell was supposed to have occurred. Much has been written over the years, even on The Middle Stump website last year, and no one really knows what happened, apart from Ian Chappell doing the Del Shannon, otherwise known as a 'Runaway'!

Good performances for Somerset followed, and in July 1977 Botham made his first of 102 Test appearances against Australia, bowling Greg Chappell, brother of Ian, for his first Test wicket. It was during this time that he wore the mitten-type gloves as modelled by every 1970s cricketing fashionista. St Peter made these and they were popular with the likes of Tony Greig around this time. I really wanted a pair as a kid and they were the cutting edge of cricketing apparel in the Silver Jubilee summer, along with the flared, bell-bottomed white flannels.

Beefy's career just went skywards over the next few years and until 1980, he was outstanding. A total of 202 Test wickets at

21.20 per wicket at this stage in his career was up there with the greats such as Marshall and Ambrose, and when you put it into context, it was better than McGrath, Warne or Murali – it just goes to show what an outstanding bowler he was in this period, before back injuries, the odd pint and the odd cigar took their toll. If you chuck in a batting average of 38.80 from his first 51 Test matches, along with numerous slip catches, it just adds to the legend and talisman that he became for England.

In 1980 he scored a hundred against India and took 100 wickets. Not many seam bowlers picked up a ten-fer in India around this time, let alone scored a ton in the same match. He picked up a 'Michelle Pfeiffer' (five-fer) and scored a ton in the same match on five occasions. No one else has done this more than twice. Words, let alone statistics, cannot describe what an outstanding cricketer Botham was for England during the late 1970s.

The next step was the England captaincy in 1980. It was tough that Botham had back-to-back series with the best side in the world in the West Indies to contend with, but a record of no wins in thirteen meant this all came to an end at Lord's in the 1981 Ashes. This was when the membership of the MCC disgracefully turned their back on him, in his last innings as skipper, when he was bowled around his legs by Ray Bright for a pair.

We all know what happened in the next match at Headingley, and as a child I remember coming home from school as an 11 year old and watching the evening session on BBC2 as Beefy, Graham 'Picca' Dilley and Chris 'Chilly' Old gave it some long lever. It was one of the best innings I have ever seen from an Englishman, for defiance and just an amazing knock. A total of 149 not out, and England won a game they had followed on in!

Five wickets for one run to win the next Test at Edgbaston, followed by a ton at Old Trafford and a national hero was back! Nothing epitomises that series more than Beefy slapping an Aussie bowler straight back at him, and the bowler cowering with his hands on his head in his follow through, such was the strength of Botham's hitting. I have a feeling it was Lillee or Alderman. Maybe it was both?

At this point there was nothing Botham couldn't do. A hole in one at the Belfry, playing football for Scunthorpe United or Yeovil Town, writing off a couple of Saabs in one day, pissing it up with a large cigar in his hand – you can see why he was a magnet for the tabloid press, in the unregulated days of the 1980s, when the Leveson inquiry was merely a twinkle in the eye of the beholder. It soon went wrong. Tabloid tales aplenty, and some of what went on was way below what a family man representing his country at sport should have to contend with, especially when they would try and ask his kids about him, or what Daddy had had for lunch.

In the later years Botham's career wasn't up there with the way it had started, although he remained a bowler who could pick up wickets, sometimes even just via reputation. Some he gained through his ability to swing the ball and some were just simply conned – victims of daylight robbery. A total of 383 wickets in Test matches wasn't a bad haul.

In 1986, civil war erupted in Somerset when the infamous acrimonious battle of Shepton Mallet (which in fact was actually an AGM) occurred, and lifelong friends Richards and Garner were sacked from Somerset with man-of-principle Botham following them by resigning. A lifelong dislike of Peter Roebuck, counsel for the other side, followed.

Botham then played for Queensland, generally to escape the 'English red tops', but was sacked for giving a fellow airline passenger the benefit of his advice, and a spell at Worcestershire followed. Worcester were a top-drawer side at the time, thanks to the rather generous contracts given by Duncan Fearnley to Dilley, Hick, Botham and the like, and New Road was awash with silverware – in the days when it wasn't awash with the River Severn.

He completed his wonderful career at Durham. Since then, he has embarked on walks, such as John O'Groats to Land's End and across Europe, in aid of Leukaemia Research. He has raised over £12 million for charity, which is worthy of a knighthood alone.

He will be remembered as an outstanding competitor and one of the finest all-rounders ever, in a generation remembered for some outstanding all-rounders. Look at the likes of Kapil Dev, Imran Khan, Sir Richard Hadlee and Clive Rice, who all hailed from this generation. Some very fine cricketers indeed there, and Botham was up there with them, trading to be the main man for your team. Allied to the fact he would make things happen, ignite a game and had the whole country talking about him in pubs at times in his career, Beefy was a national treasure. He was a popular man, unless you lived in the Roebuck, Boycott or Chappell houses, or were Imran Khan, who had a couple of post-career duels with him in the High Court in the 1990s. A knighthood followed for services to his country and he is now a commentator for Sky.

I like Beefy's style. He is honest, says what he thinks and no doubt probably gets up the noses of a few Australians whilst commentating. I shouldn't imagine it will bother him though. He's only been doing it for nearly forty years!

WHATCHA TALKING 'BOUT, WILLIS?

Looking back to 1981, Botham would have been nothing, though, had it not been for a spell of fast bowling at Headingley that was just quite simply amazing. England, down and out, were 500–1 to win the match with some bookies and although everyone remembers it for Botham's knock, another man ensured that the victory, and some may say the series, happened. That man was Robert George Dylan Willis.

Born in Sunderland but brought up in Surrey, Big Bob Willis joined his native county in the summer of 1969 as a promising fast bowler. At 6ft 6in tall, and a right handful, he was soon picked for England and toured Australia in 1971 under Ray Illingworth, as a late replacement. Willis recalled that Illy and Cowdrey knew nothing about him, and he was picked purely on the recommendation of Surrey stalwart, John Edrich. Maybe it was because he shared a similar hairstyle to John Snow?

The Oval wasn't a happy place in the early 1970s, and Mike Selvey departed for Middlesex whilst Willis found pastures new in Birmingham. Not many bowlers had a run-up as long as Willis at the time, maybe Mikey Holding apart, and it has to be said that I have travelled less distances on my holidays. Bob started becoming an excellent bowler for England, but not so much for Warwickshire, and it was during the middle part of this decade that he missed a lot of games through injury. He also had the name 'Dylan' added by deed poll in recognition of his favourite songwriter, another Bob (Dylan).

Injuries were a thorn in his side, no doubt due to his action, but he was still too quick for the Aussies in 1977, and was named Cricketer of the Year in 1978.

Towards the end of the 1970s he pinned a couple of batsmen quite nastily. With his arms whirling and a fairly ugly action, he was big, he was intimidating and thank fuck he was English!

Rick McCosker was the first one, not only getting his jaw broken in the Centenary Test, but also getting bowled from the same delivery. Now that's unlucky. McCosker was strapped up like an Egyptian mummy for the rest of the game, and no doubt had to have his dinner through a straw for months to come. Rick McCosker? Rick MaCosted more like.

The other one was more controversial in 1978. Iqbal Qasim was a poor batsman, but sent in as nightwatchman he hung around annoying England for forty minutes, until Bob banged one in at him. Unable to cope with the sheer pace, the ball clattered the unfortunate Qasim straight in the gob and the Pakistani started producing more claret than a Bordeaux vineyard. Pakistan and their management went nuts during play as poor old Iqbal visited the dentist, having had his teeth rearranged in a similar way to the furniture when you have a row with the missus. Tail-enders were still under the code of conduct not to be bounced back then, but technically he was batting at No. 3. It was after this that 'lids' started to prevail.

More injuries followed and in 1981, with England 1–0 down to Australia, Willis was actually dropped for the Headingley Test, having bowled a mammoth twenty-eight no-balls at Lord's. Pakistanis have visited English prisons for less. For some reason he came back in having had a chat with Alec Bedser, and this was his finest moment. After Botham's heroic 149, aided by the not-to-be-forgotten knock of 52 from the now sadly deceased Graham Dilley, England had given themselves a glimmer of hope, setting the Aussies 130.

Willis, steaming down the hill from the Kirkstall Lane end, just bounced all of the Aussie batsmen out bar Dennis Lillee and was in the zone. He hardly even celebrated the wickets, and his eyes were equivalent to that of a mass murderer, staring wildly like he was on drugs. Even the rioters of Toxteth and Brixton at the time in that summer of 1981 would have crapped themselves at Willis that day. Never mind the Scarman Report, the Metropolitan Police should have just called up 'Big Bad Bob'. He finished by uprooting Ray Bright's middle stump and finished with 8–43 in one of the finest displays of bowling I have ever witnessed.

The captaincy followed, and I remember it more for his monotone, monosyllabic interviews during this era, and you wonder how did he ever make it into the commentary box? He finished up in 1984 with 325 Test wickets, at the time, only second in the world behind Lillee. He will be remembered as one of the finest fast bowlers of his generation, of which there were plenty, and he often bowled through the pain barrier for his country.

A career in commentating soon followed, and this is where Willis has been at his most controversial. Highly critical, especially of England after a poor display, Willis pulls no punches and is the hatchet man of the studio. Mike Atherton, Michael Vaughan, Duncan Fletcher, Kevin Pietersen (described as the 'dumbslog millionaire') and many more, have been on his hit list, and even recently, claims that England were ball-tampering, were highly controversial. Like David Icke, another sporting man who has gone from the '70s perm to a straight-haired 60-year-old plus, shocking the public comes easy to Willis and controversy is rarely a stranger.

Willis regularly had trouble sleeping when he was a player, so much so that he regularly took tablets. His languid style has been described as struggling to stay awake in the commentary box, and it has also been described as that of a high-pitched monotone mower!

I like Willis, though, and he adds colour to our screens. He is forthright – you never know what is going to come out of his mouth, especially when England have played badly. He makes a great pundit back in the studio, and you always want to hear what he has to say when we have been hammered.

Bob Willis, you're mad as a March hare, but you are most definitely one of our characters of cricket.

BLINDING BUMBLE

David Lloyd has lived and breathed cricket since his birth in March 1947, and is an integral part of the British summer. Our second favourite son of Accrington (Foxy Fowler being the first), here is a rundown on the career of the man, universally known and loved as 'Bumble'. Lloyd has morphed throughout his career: a spinner on debut, he then opened the batting for his country, before a career in umpiring, coaching and now commentary all beckoned.

Lloyd was an all-rounder, a decent left-arm bat and an underrated spinner who made his debut for Lancashire in 1965, unfortunately bagging a pair against Middlesex. In 1968 he scored his first hundred, and in 1970, 1971 and 1972 he won the Gillette Cup in an era when Lancashire were the kings of One Day cricket. He also bagged over 1,000 runs in each of these seasons, and was soon made captain. You could see his enthusiasm for the game already, and this is what has led to a lifetime in cricket.

Promotion to the England team followed, and his debut was the famous Test match that England won by the small margin of an innings and 285 runs, as Geoff Arnold and Chris 'Chilly' Old bowled India out for just 42 – for some of us that is a waist size, not an innings total. In the next match at Edgbaston, Lloyd scored a stylish 214 not out as they put India to the sword yet again.

He was then unfortunate enough to meet Lillee and Thommo in their pomp in Australia, and was battered out of the tour, and ultimately Test cricket. One look at YouTube sees Bumble get hit in the winkle, and he ends up on the deck for nearly as long as Rip Van Winkle. Boxes back in those days were those thin, pink, plastic things not much bigger than a sewing thimble, and allegedly the crown jewels of Accrington were forced through the small holes designed to give air to one's pubic region (or in Australia, to keep the flies away from your vegemite sarnie)!

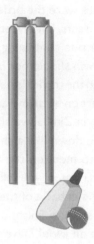

He only played 9 Tests averaging over 42, in an era where 42 is today's 52. The likes of Lillee, Thommo, Roberts, Holding and Co. ensured that only the elite averaged over 50 in this decade. In an era of financial struggle for the UK, the run had been devalued and inflation of bowlers' wickets soared.

Lloyd was recalled to the ODI side in 1978 and 1980, albeit not hugely successfully. Bumble himself says he should never have been recalled, and blames it on the bad captaincy of Ian Botham! The Lancashire dressing room sounds like my sort of place in the early 1980s, with anecdotes a plenty, from Frank Hayes' refuelling habits; to Jack Simmons' penchant for food; the two Lloyds – Clive and David – with their afro hairstyles; and Bumble was at the heart of a lot of the japes. His humour is an integral part of the man, and although having never met him, I'm sure he would be great value over a pint or two.

After his retirement in 1983, Lloyd was a first-class umpire for a couple of years but, it not really being his cup of tea, he moved into coaching. He took the role of coach at his beloved Red Rose county before England came calling in 1996.

Churchillian speeches were the order of the day, and despite the lack of central contracts, England still managed to beat South Africa in 1998. With a side containing Kallis, Klusener, Donald, Pollock and Co., this win should not be underestimated in the start of England's rise to the top in the early millennium. A popular coach, he wore his heart on his sleeve and the famous 'We flippin' murdered 'em!' quote in Zimbabwe showed the passion of the man. It may have gone down like a shit sandwich with the hoi polloi at Lord's, not to mention the locals in Zimbabwe, but when you are from Accrington, you tell it how it is.

He resigned after the debacle of the 1999 World Cup, which was a shambles from start to finish, on and off the pitch. Only England could release an awful Dave Stewart song which was nothing about cricket the day after we got knocked out of the tournament. Alec Stewart could have penned a better track.

Now a commentator on Sky, everyone loves the avuncular Bumble and we all love his anecdotes. He describes his life in cricket as 'having a laugh, coincidentally with cricket involved', and that makes him a hero, not just to Englishmen, but to cricket fans around the globe. In his excellent book, *Start the Car*, he mentions a time in India when he was told by one Indian fan that he was his favourite commentator. After a load of photos, Bumble made his excuses and left and the Indian chap replied, 'Thank you, Mr Paul Arlott!' Saying that, in India he has been confused with Tony Greig, Duncan Fletcher, Darrell Hair and even Bruce Yardley!

Sometimes, working for Sky commentating on games broadcast by other countries' cameramen can provide some of the more interesting moments, though. In South Africa, a couple of chaps were sitting down eating watermelon and Bumble commented on those delicious melons. Unbeknown to him, the camera had panned around to a rather buxom young lady in the crowd!

On Twitter, too, he is accessible, answering questions, and often those of a banal nature with good humour. He likes the accessibility to players via the media, as do we here, and one of the reasons we have been successful getting some great interviews for The Middle Stump is that cricketers are far more accessible and friendly than in other sports. Bumble is an integral part of that and some of his 'Tweets of the Roses' with resident Yorkshire tweeter Fred Boycott have been hilarious.

He is also well into his music, and a huge fan of Mark E. Smith, Inspiral Carpets and The Fall. Another delve into YouTube finds him giving it the large one to 'Saturn 5' by the Inspirals as they played during a rain break at Old Trafford. Even mad Lancashire cricket fan, Middle Stump interviewee and guitarist of Inspiral Carpets, Graham Lambert, gives him a nod at one point. Kudos.

We hope that Bumble is on our screens for many more years to come. He is the John Arlott of the modern age, with that distinctive Accrington voice coming across, just like Arlott's Hampshire gravelly burr did in the 1970s. I often get the impression that when he says 'flippin'' he actually very nearly swears on air but changes it from 'fuck' to 'flip' at the last second.

For that, the cricketing world loves Bumble.

BRACEWELL, THE BLOB

I have seen some horrendous collapses in my time. The roof of the Apollo Theatre, Tommy Cooper sliding down the curtain at the Royal Variety Show, or Richard Dunn's legs after his fight with Muhammad Ali in the 1970s all spring to mind. We wonder, though, if there will be such a poor performance with the bat, in any series, as the one we saw back in 1978. We look back at the scores of a certain Brendon Bracewell on that tour and it makes interesting reading.

Bracewell was one of four cricketing brothers, and was picked on this tour as an up-and-coming, raw 18-year-old quick. In the first Test at the Oval, Brendon, batting at the elevated heights of No. 10, managed to get a duck on debut. Nothing unusual about that, shall we say? It has happened to finer players such as the likes of Graham Gooch.

Young Brendon then opened the bowling, and removed England's opening pair of Brearley and Gooch in quick succession before the first of numerous Test hundreds from a 21-year-old David Gower lit up south London.

In the second knock, the Kiwis disintegrated with our friend Master Bracewell recording a pair, bowled by that wizard of off-spin, Geoff Miller. Maybe he thought that Geoff's pace was 'Greased Lightning' (one of the tracks from the most popular film of that year) because he certainly wasn't 'Hopelessly Devoted' to batting. England knocked the runs off easily in the second dig to win by 7 wickets.

On to Nottingham, and the 'home' ground of Richard Hadlee. A painfully slow 131 from Geoffrey Boycott underpinned England's 429 before 6 wickets from Beefy sorted out the Kiwis. Our friend Brendon, now demoted to No. 11, got a duck, but in mitigation he did manage to last eight balls this time. When they followed on they didn't fare much better, and although Brendon didn't trouble the scorers again, he did manage a not out.

Another thing I recall from this series would be the commentators on the BBC at the time. The shining, or should that be sheening, pate of Peter West's bonce would introduce the series, and they seriously built up a couple of the Kiwis who were, in truth, fucking awful. Bev Congdon and the slogging keeper, Jock Edwards, are just a couple who spring to my ageing mind. Anderson, their opener, was another walking wicket.

The final Test at Lord's, and New Zealand actually took the lead in the first innings. A classy 123 from Surrey stalwart

Geoff Howarth was the mainstay of their total, going through the pain barrier with piles. You could say he was the southern hemisphere John Steinbeck, as his 'grapes of wrath' were seriously dangling, so much so that he almost didn't bat in the second knock. Even Brendon chipped in, edging one through the slips for 4 before getting stumped by Bob Taylor off John Emburey.

A total of 70-odd from Clive Radley and David Gower were not enough to close the gap, and England were looking at chasing a problematic score in the fourth dig before New Zealand were skittled for a mere 67. Howarth was batting at No. 9 due to his 'Emma Freuds', and Hadlee, for some reason or other, batted at No. 10. Richie Collinge must have been seriously shite as Bracewell went up to No. 8 in the order. He reverted to type, by getting a third ball blob.

England won the series 3–0, thanks to 40s from Gower and Gooch, but it was Brendon Bracewell that lived in the memory bank for me in that summer of 1978. John Travolta was what all the other kids were talking about at school, or the emerging Glenn Hoddle. Pah! For me it was Brendon. The ironic cheers whenever he blocked a forward defensive and, with a grand total of 4 runs, squirted through the slips via one scoring shot in six knocks in that series, we can only say – Brendon Bracewell, for this reason alone, you are one of the characters of cricket.

Let's hope his son Doug has a better career with the bat …

1981 - WHEN THE GAME WAS FULL OF CHARACTERS

Clearing out some old books recently, I came across the fine publication that was *The Cricketer's Who's Who* from 1981. The year that Botham bashed the Aussies threw up some fine childhood memories, including some absolutely howling haircuts. Questions such as 'why did the average county cricketer enjoy the Peter Sutcliffe look?' spring to mind, or whether Mike Bore was smoking some 'wicked shit' to get his eyes into that sort of state, or the numerous cricketers who played in glasses at that time ... the book is now my bible and I cannot put it down.

Bill Merry's mullet is probably up there for the worst haircut in the book, but Bumble with a perm takes some beating, it has to be said! Keith Jennings of Somerset has a particularly shocking 'do', as does Arthur Francis of Glamorgan. John Birch of Nottinghamshire looks rather too similar to the photo they always used to trot out of Myra Hindley for my liking, you know the peroxide one? Alan Lilley could easily pass for her partner in crime, Ian Brady, for that matter. The now departed Peter Denning prefers the straggly look, and could do with borrowing a wig from his namesake, Justice Denning.

The perm seemed de rigueur in the Midlands at the time amongst the fast bowling fraternity, and high fashionistas such as Paul Pridgeon at Worcester, Bob Willis at Warwickshire and Gordon Parsons at Leicester, all sported the curls. Amongst the Kevins, the afro perm seemed more popular, with Brooks at Derbyshire and Sharp at Yorkshire looking like the long lost albino members of the Stylistics! David Surridge sports the look of one of the most famous people of that year ... Lady Diana Spencer.

Glamorgan, meanwhile, just had the three players called 'Alan' or 'Allan' Jones, so no doubt there was confusion aplenty down at Sophia Gardens at the time, long before it was the SWALEC.

Local legend Alan Jones had just notched up his twentieth year in a row to score 1,000 runs, whilst Allan Jones, having arrived in Cardiff via Middlesex, Sussex and Somerset, was the Maria Sharapova of the bowling world, renowned for delivering a hideous grunting sound, akin to the mating call of the rhinoceros. Alan Lewis Jones was also profiled in this fine piece of cricketing literature, and Alan (not Allan, not Alan Lewis) had a brother called Eifion just to complete the dream scorecard of the lazy scorer. Barry Jones of Worcester completes the Jones section. This was, however, in the days before Adrian Jones of Sussex, who once suffered from a horrendous no-balling problem. One of the more senior Sussex members cried out aghast, 'Oh come on Jones!', before the Sussex paceman yelled out from over 50 yards away, 'Come down here then if you can fucking well do any better!' Needless to say he had to find employment elsewhere shortly afterwards.

Naturally for a book of this era, there are tashes aplenty, with five in a row at one point in the 'O's. Chris Old of Yorkshire; Steve Oldham, then at Derbyshire; Martin Olive of Somerset; Phil Oliver at Warwickshire, with Rodney Ontong completing the full house. Only Ormerod and O'Shaughnessy ruin the perfect score for top lip slugs, and I'm sure they sported facial fuzz later, or maybe earlier, in their careers! Maybe these were the cricketing equivalent of Liverpool FC at the time. Alan Butcher, meanwhile, the father of England batsman, Mark, has some outrageous 'sideys', obviously the cutting edge of fashion at that point in south London.

Nottinghamshire players look seriously fucking hard. Kevin Saxelby looks like he could punch your lights out, while John Birch could well run the roost in a moody boozer on the Meadows Estate in Nottingham. Birch looks more like someone found drinking in a council estate pub on a Monday lunchtime, or one of the numerous individuals who have given me a hard time on my visits to northern towns, for no other reason than I support a London football club, as opposed to a professional cricketer. John Barclay, a man with a middle man of Troutbeck, he is most certainly not.

Back at Notts, Mike Harris also looks a bruiser, as does Paul Todd, whilst Peter Graves down at Sussex does a more than passable impression of 'Razors', Bob Hoskins' sidekick and henchman in the film *The Long Good Friday*. How a bloke with a glass eye ever played the professional game, I don't know, although Chris Tavare's knocks against the Aussies that year would have almost certainly sent Graves' glass eye to sleep.

The other odd thing is players leaving their address and telephone number at the bottom of their page. Most of them, to be fair, put c/o their county cricket club, but numerous high-profile names leaving their own personal address and number seemed strange to say the least. I'm sure Imran Khan, now a politician in Pakistan, has learned to be a tad more security conscious than the days when he lived in Eaton Road, Hove.

Unfortunately, I cannot open the last few pages as I believe I no doubt spilt some Five Alive (remember that?) so the book finishes at Stephen Windaybank of Gloucestershire, and the papyrus seems to be stuck together.

All in all, a cracking read and my knowledge of early 1980s cricketers is now one to behold.

GLADSTONE SMALL - THE BAJAN BRUMMIE

Ian Botham is sitting down in an Australian restaurant with Rod Marsh and Dennis Lillee, and they have all ordered the turtle soup. After an hour they still haven't been served, and Marsh pipes up to the waiter, 'Hey mate, why hasn't our grub arrived yet?' The waiter says, 'We're terribly sorry sir, but we seem to have a bit of a problem in the kitchen with the turtle'. Beefy says 'Leave this to me' and trots off into the kitchen, followed by the two Aussies. He wets his finger, pops it into where the sun doesn't shine, out pops the turtle's head and down comes the chef's cleaver, chopping off the head of the reptile. Fifteen minutes later they are all eating their turtle soup. Lillee says to Botham, 'That's a great trick mate, where did you learn that?' to which Ian replies, 'Oh, it is an old one in the England dressing room. How do you think we get Gladstone Small's tie on every morning!'

However, there was much more to Gladstone Small than the old after-dinner circuit joke. He arrived in England as a 14 year old, and applied personally to the MCC to play for England as opposed to his native Barbados, where he would have qualified for the West Indies. The story goes that they took one look at this young lad who looked like he had swallowed a coat hanger, along with his spectacles, and thought that he wouldn't get to play for England, so granted him permission.

A sufferer of Klippel-Feil syndrome, where the bones in the vertebrae are fused, giving the distinctive look of having no neck, Small overcame many obstacles early in his career but had the sense to switch from an out-and-out paceman into a great away swing bowler.

When he first came on to the scene in 1982, Small had a nightmare against Middlesex in a match at Coventry. He bowled an 18-ball over when he overstepped the mark ten times. This he tried to combat by bowling off a couple of paces and ended up slipping in a wide. However, he showed the character to overcome such obstacles, and international recognition followed.

He became one of the top characters of the game, and a recent interview with the musician Eggsy from Goldie Lookin Chain brought up the subject of Gladstone. Eggsy, a son of Newport in South Wales played many a cricket match at Valleys grounds in the freezing cold, and kids from this region would perfect 'doing the Gladstone'. This involved them being so cold when neither batting nor bowling, that they would be hunched up with their head down in their shoulders to protect them from the elements. Many kids who were there just to make up the numbers would be 'doing the Gladstone'.

'Gladys', as he was known, was the star of the Melbourne Test on the famous 'can't bat, can't bowl, can't field' tour of 1986/87. Having been named as a last-minute call up, he took 5 Australian wickets in the first innings on Boxing Day in front of a packed MCG, with Ian Botham taking the other 5 wickets. He then contributed a hard-hitting 21 not out in the lower order, before removing the top order and catching Merv Hughes in the deep off the bowling of Phil Edmonds to ensure that England retained the Ashes. Just for good measure, he gave their middle order a good going over a week later in Sydney!

What we loved about Gladstone was that he tried his arse off. Not only did we like him but *everyone* did. Imagine a retro-Monty mania, such as when Panesar came on the scene, and that is what you had with Small. A great team man, he was a member of the England World Cup sides of both 1987 and 1992 – sides that narrowly missed out in both finals. In between, he also took 8 West Indian wickets on the island where he was born in 1989/90. This was the West Indies of Viv Richards and Richie Richardson, and although not as strong as a few years previously, they were still a far greater force than they are now, and still No. 1 in the world.

With the England selection policy the way it was, not many players escaped the selector's axe, and Gladstone was no exception to the rule. He was part of the fine Warwickshire side of 1994 who won the treble under Bob Woolmer, and after retirement became a director of the Professional Cricketers' Association. One of the most popular cricketers on the circuit is now a renowned after-dinner speaker, and apparently a bloody good one at that.

As they used to sing at Edgbaston to the tune of the Lambeth Walk:

> Any evening any day
> When you're down Warwick way
> You'll find us all
> Doing the Gladstone Small

With the movement of them hunching their shoulders up for the last line. Gladys loved it and is truly a real character of cricket.

BAD BOYS XI

Here is a list of some of cricket's bad boys. It features the players who aren't listed elsewhere in this book but each deserve their place in this side. Some are worse than others …

DAVID WARNER

An explosive batsman both on and off the field, Davey Warner's disciplinary problems throughout 2013 nearly killed off his international career. Already in trouble with New South Wales for missing a match, his tirade at Australian journalists over Twitter were merely the hors d'oeuvres when he came to notice for punching Joe Root in Walkabout in Birmingham at 2 a.m., because the Yorkshireman had donned a fake beard. Let's hope he prefers to punch through the covers as opposed to the opposition's jawline in future.

SALMAN BUTT

The Pakistan captain who ordered his players to bowl no-balls in return for large sums of money. Butt was caught in a sting by the *News of the World* and received thirty months in a British jail for his troubles. Banned from the game for ten years too, it is unknown whether the Butt was no-balled whilst in Wormwood Scrubs.

HERSCHELLE GIBBS

The South African opener famously blubbed through the King Commission into match fixing, claiming he had been offered $15,000 to score less than 20 runs. Gibbs went and scored 74, and as a result was only banned for six months for his part in the sordid affair. For some reason, Gibbs was terrified to tour India soon afterwards, fearing arrest or, no doubt, those who had gambled on him previously to score less than 20 runs. Gibbs was then caught on a stump mike telling Pakistani fans to 'go back to the zoo', and banned. Throw in getting caught smoking a spliff and getting fined in the Windies in 2001, Gibbs' form is certainly worse than that which led to his career going down the pan.

HANSiE CRONJE

Possibly the worst one of the lot. Cronje used his position as captain of South Africa to ensure that there was a result in the Test match at Centurion v. England in 1999, for, apparently, a leather jacket. Implicated in the King Inquiry with Gibbs, Nicky Boje and Pieter Strydom, Gibbs was banned from Test cricket.

Killed in a plane crash in 2002 in South Africa, many have thought that other theories abounded – such as retribution from gambling syndicates – despite the inquest saying it was accidental. The sudden death of Bob Woolmer, South Africa's coach at the time, has only enhanced these whispers.

MOHAMMAD AZHARUDDiN

The man who Cronje named as introducing him to the dodgy bookies, Azha was one of the most beautiful batsmen to watch in world cricket. Wristy and elegant, India mourned when he was banned for life by the BCCI in 2000. Again, a family member was killed in mysterious circumstances when his son died in a motorbike accident. Azha's life ban was lifted recently, and now he is in that profession of all those with a decent conscience – politics.

MOHAMMAD ASiF

Shoaib Akhtar's bat mallet, as he was known when the Rawalpindi Express tried to hit him with the willow, has a record as long as Joel Garner's arm. Nandrolone, recreational doping, fighting with teammates, you name it, he's done it. A spell at Leicestershire was full of spats with the opposition, and one gentleman who played against him has privately admitted to us that he urinated in his ice bath before the end of play due to the disgraceful attitude of the Pakistani seamer. Part of Salman Butt's spot-fixing trio, he spent six months behind bars in Canterbury before borrowing money off his model girlfriend and then bouncing cheques when she demanded the money back. A veritable prince among men by the sounds of things.

DAVID MURRAY

Now living in abject poverty in Barbados, Rastafarian Murray was described by Michael Holding as the best wicketkeeper of all time. Having admitted to smoking weed since the age of 12, Murray turned to cocaine in India and was nearly sent home after rowing with Bernard Julien over his habits. The son of Sir Everton Weekes lost his place to namesake Deryck Murray and went off on a rebel tour to South Africa, before being banned for life.

COLIN CROFT

Now a respected journalist, Croft was a pilot during his stint with the West Indies of the 1970s. A man who would go wide on the crease and use the angles to terrify batsmen, Croft's patience finally snapped in New Zealand in 1980. After an incident which caused even the placid Mikey Holding to boot the stumps down, Croft had had enough of the umpires and the 6ft 5in quick decided to deliberately barge one in his run-up. Another one to tour South Africa and receive a hefty ban for his troubles.

SHOAIB AKHTAR

Rows with teammates have dogged this Pakistani quick throughout his tumultuous career, but hitting Mohammad Asif with a bat caused the most controversy. Regularly fined for breaching team curfews, the 'Rawalpindi Express' also sued the Pakistani Cricket Board for releasing information that he was suffering from genital warts. Steroids have been another controversy, although he was cleared of using them. Other bans for abusing players and ball-tampering have dogged his career. One of the few bowlers in world cricket to have topped 100mph, Akhtar has played for numerous English counties without much success.

HARBHAJAN SiNGH

'The Turbanator' was an ex-police officer in India, but this didn't stop him from getting into a brawl with some of the local constabulary in 2002, having been expelled from his country's academy in his younger years. He was banned later in his career for allegedly calling Andrew Symonds 'a monkey', which led to Matthew Hayden calling him an 'obnoxious weed' in response. Both were disciplined for their troubles.

'Bhajji' was later banned from the IPL for hitting his India teammate Sreesanth across the face, losing his salary. Other controversies include advertising whisky without his turban, which almost led to riots amongst the more orthodox Sikhs in his community.

DENNiS LiLLEE

Quite possibly the finest bowler of all time was no stranger when it came to the verbals. Using language of an industrial nature blighted his early career, before he went off to find his fortune with Kerry Packer. On his return, he had a massive row with Mike Brearley over using an aluminium bat which was manufactured by a friend of his, with the England captain claiming he was damaging the ball.

In 1981, he bet on his own side to lose in the Headingley Test at odds of 500–1, which would earn him a lifetime ban these days. In 1982, he kicked Javed Miandad, before the Pakistani threatened to wrap his bat (this time made of willow) around his head.

TONY GREIG

> Give your hand to cricket and it will take you on the most fantastic
> journey, a lifetime journey both on and off the field.
>
> *A.W. Grieg, 2012*

Tony Greig, who passed away in December 2012 in Sydney, was an innovator. Whether it be trying to organise a break away from the TCCB under the media mogul Kerry Packer, wearing his collar up long before a certain footballing Frenchman in Manchester made it popular, the curved run to the stumps with blond locks flowing, or his trademark St Peter gloves, he did things his way.

Controversy tended to follow the man with a Scottish father and a South African mother, and in 1974 he upset the 'Trini Posse' by running out Alvin Kallicharran, having pretended to walk off the pitch with him at the end of the day's play. Kalli was given out by Jamaican umpire, Douglas Sang Hue, and the Trini Posse went 'radio rental', with the Old Bill being sent in to the crowd to quell the uprising with their sticks. Greig wisely withdrew his appeal after a couple of hours, having decided he fancied getting out of Port of Spain alive!

He wound up Dennis Lillee in the famous whipping England took in Australia in 1974/75 (sounds like a Connells' track, doesn't it?) He did score a brilliant ton in the first Test in Brisbane, and was one of the few players who came out of that tour with his reputation intact. Thommo and Lillee gave the English batting a thorough going over, but Greig stood firm against a pace battery.

After the 1975 World Cup, England sacked Mike Denness and Greig took over as captain, although the Sussex man had to concede the Ashes after vandals, who were supporters of alleged bank robber George Davis, destroyed the pitch in an effort to highlight his unsafe conviction. (Davis was subsequently cleared, although convicted of a different charge for a similar offence just a few months later.) With England in a strong position, these followers of Davis were about as popular as a Man United fan in Leeds. Let's say the supporters of George Davis did more for Aussie chances than namesake and walking wicket Ian Davis did a few years later. Just to keep up with the Aussie coincidences, one of the pitch saboteurs was called Chappell.

In 1976, Greig was again in the news for vowing to make the touring West Indians 'grovel'. With the South African overtones (a country who employed the nefarious system of apartheid at the time), this comment was at its best, insensitive. With no further motivation needed, Holding, Daniel, Roberts and Co. gave the English batting a serious working over, and Greig was left looking rather silly.

His last Test as skipper was the one-off Centenary Test in 1977, and although England lost by 45 runs, Greig won many friends in Australia, a country he was eventually to settle in. After organising some of the best players in the world to play in the Kerry Packer-inspired World Series, Greig was removed from the captaincy, although he was surprisingly retained to play against the Aussies under Mike Brearley.

Greig was vastly unpopular in the Jubilee year, putting money ahead of his country, but cricketers had been extremely poorly paid up until this time, and this set the standard for the sums floating around in the international game now. In later years, he was to play a similarly prominent role in Indian T20 cricket – another money-spinning venture.

After playing in the World Series, Greig, controversial to the end, promised his fans a century in his last game but failed by a hundred runs as he was caught off the bowling of his nemesis, Dennis Lillee. A career including eight Test hundreds and a best bowling performance of 8–86 had come to an end.

His post-playing career was in commentary for Channel Nine in Australia, and he was a regular here, poking his key into the pitch with his wide-brimmed hat. Again courting controversy, he landed in hot water in 2006, after a camera zoomed in on a wedding, and tactful Tony asked, 'Do you think she has been flown in?', implying that the oriental-looking bride was of the mail-order variety.

He would regularly talk about a batsman being strong through the 'orf side' and thank God he never had to commentate on the football from the former Wankdorf Stadium in Berne!

An epileptic, Greig was diagnosed with lung cancer a few months before passing away from a heart attack. Whether you were a fan of his or not – and his popularity seemed to split the cricketing world – you cannot argue that cricket has lost one of the great characters of the game, an innovator, and one who stood up and was counted when the going got tough.

Anthony William Greig, rest in peace.

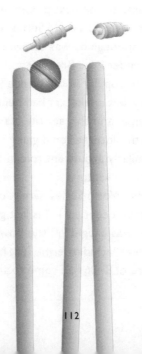

TAVARE THE TORTOISE

Almost thirty years ago, the Australian fast bowler Geoff Lawson bowled his umpteenth delivery to Chris Tavare, the English batsman. Tav pushed it into the covers and called 'Waiting' to the non-striker Graeme Fowler. Lawson turned around and said, 'Mate, we're always fucking waiting!' This is how most people look back on the career of Chris Tavare, but there was more in his repertoire than just the block.

He may have had a name similar to a French rugby three-quarter, the type synonymous with panache, grace and élan, but it was only for England that this Basil Fawlty lookalike blocked in the 1980s like a French union worker on strike at Dieppe. Replace the Australian bowling attack with an English lorry driver trying to get home and you'll get a sense of how frustrating a player Tavare was.

Having graduated with a degree in zoology from Oxford in the mid-1970s, and having studied the tortoise for his dissertation along with a loris, a snail and a sloth, maybe, Tav was a sparkling, reasonably quick-scoring middle order batsman for his native Kent. He was even known to outscore the likes of Asif Iqbal in the middle order. Even when he was brought into the England team in 1980 for his debut, he wasn't too bad, but it was in his tête-à-tête with the 1981 Australians that Tav came into his own. A change of grip to a bottom-handed defensive one to combat some of the genuine speed merchants around at the time, which nullified his scoring shots, was the source of many a wasted hour for me watching as a child.

It was during this series that a marathon 69 and 78, spanned over a mere twelve hours, brought him to the forefront of the English slow hand-clappers. One gentleman from the crowd even brought out a deck chair on to the arena. Harsh indeed, considering he was just doing a job for the team so the likes of Gooch, Gower and

Botham could then play their shots. The antithesis of stroke play, 'Tav the Tortoise' blocked one end, whilst the hare-like Botham smashed it at the other. Watching it as a kid, you knew you could have a toilet break when it was Tavare's turn to face, but you didn't want to miss a moment of Botham's knock.

He was described by a journalist once as, 'for Tavare, scoring runs seemed a disagreeable, even vulgar distraction from the pure art of surviving'. After every block he also had a habit of walking off towards square leg, having a word with himself before showing us the next forward defensive. He drove every non-Englishman nuts.

After the Australian series, Tavare scored 35 in nearly a day in India. A turgid knock standing out in a turgid series, there were even jokes going around like the one with an Indian teacher asking her pupils the meaning of the word 'contagious'. Firstly, little Sunil puts his hand up and says, 'Miss, if I have a cold I mustn't come to school as I might be contagious'. Next, Anil puts his hand up and says, 'Miss, my mum says I have to wash my hands if I have been around Sunil with a cold as I may be contagious'. The teacher tells them they are very good, when little Sanjay at the back shouts out, 'Miss, I watched Chris Tavare bat all day yesterday in the match at Madras. He only got 35 and it took the contagious!'

A sparkling 89 over eight hours in Perth made him as popular as prohibition with the Australian crowds, but it was in this series that he had a revolution, a renaissance moment. Having played his usual knock at Melbourne, Tavare suddenly got bored and gave the long handle to the Aussies, Bruce Yardley in particular coming in for some punishment. He finished up with the same score as at Perth, just in about an eighth of the time! It was during this Test that Tavare dropped Jeff Thomson, the Aussie No. 11, when they needed 4 runs to win, only for Geoff Miller to pocket the rebound. An amazing finale to an amazing Test match.

Tavare lost the Kent captaincy, winding down his career at Somerset, but not before one last finale against the Australians in 1989.

Now a biology teacher back at Sevenoaks School, where he himself was educated, Christopher Tavare was indeed one of the characters of the game – even if he didn't mean to be.

EDUCATED EDMONDS

Philippe Henri Edmonds was no stranger to controversy. Not many of us have pinned England's greatest-ever captain up against the wall, but this was the treatment dished out by 'Henri' to Mike Brearley. He also did the same to no less a scribe than Simon Barnes whilst, erm, 'collaborating' on his biography. However, behind the controversy was a seriously talented cricketer, one who possibly underachieved, and one who most definitely would have had far more publicity nowadays.

The left-arm spinner had already made his mark in the early to mid-1970s on the county game, with fine performances for Middlesex and Cambridge University, where he attended Fitzwilliam College. Brearley would refer to him and Boycott as the 'Fitzwilliam twins' – Edmonds having attended the college, whilst Fiery hailed from the Yorkshire village of the same name.

On debut for England, he grabbed the headlines with a 5-wicket haul against the 1975 Aussies. However, his career stalled at international level due to being labelled 'hard work'

or 'difficult' by numerous sources. His appearances were of a sporadic nature and, despite being dubbed as the natural successor to Derek Underwood, the selectors would plump for others such as Middlesex teammate John Emburey, Geoff Miller or even Nick Cook, who were perceived as a safer pair of hands.

When we spoke to some of the Middlesex players who roomed with him around this time, they told us that Henri was popular in the dressing room, being able to dish out the stick, as well as take it. Edmonds did, however, nearly kill the Middlesex opening bat Richard Ellis once when Middlesex entertained the West Indies at Lord's. Mike Gatting had apparently nipped off for an early lunch so Ellis, being twelfth man, was stuck in at silly point to Gus Logie and Desmond Haynes – not guys known for prodding, poking or hanging around. Larry Gomes they most definitely were not. At this point Edmonds proceeded to bowl three full tosses, all of which narrowly missed Ellis, via the swishing blade of Logie. After the third one, the sub-fielder exploded, and Henri quipped, 'It was all part of a cunning plan. The only way I could have got a wicket was via a ricochet and being twelfthers, I thought you were expendable!'

He was famous, on his return from India when asked by a member of the paparazzi, 'What are you most looking forward to, being back in England?' for replying, having spent three months in the subcontinent, 'A dry fart!'

He did manage to get himself into trouble on a couple of occasions on tours to that country, and the differing reactions from the two captains were the key to handling Edmonds. David Gower, on the victorious tour in 1984/85 simply laughed off the man, also known as 'Goat', producing a copy of the *Telegraph* and reading it at square leg in response to slow scoring, a way overdue declaration from Gavaskar and a game descending into one of the most boring draws ever. Normally he preferred the *Financial Times*, we understand.

However, previously Edmonds was the recipient of one of Bob Willis' infamous glares in an earlier encounter, according to Derek Pringle. Standing at short leg, he had got into the ear of Dilip Vengsarkar and attracted the umpire's attention. Offering to go in there again when Vengsarkar batted in the second innings, he pulled the cravat he was wearing over his mouth showing that he had been gagged, turning around to show the umpire at square leg during the bowler's run up. It went down about as well as a pork pie at a bar mitzvah with the umpire, Vengsarkar and Willis!

He was no stranger to having rows with Brearley either, although Brearley spoke extremely highly of him in the *Art of Captaincy*. Edmonds was known to have walked backwards to his mark on a number of occasions just to make sure Brears didn't change the field. He was known to slip in the odd bouncer occasionally too, and remember him being warned for slipping Bruce Edgar two in a row, whilst playing for England? Not many slow left-armers can say that, now, can they?

Off the pitch Edmonds was an interesting character, too. One of cricket's first sponsorship deals, with Swatch, came his way whilst he was playing for England.

A Zambian childhood was curtailed when his father spoke out against the local white colonialists trying to emulate the brutal regime a few hundred miles further south, forcing the family to return to England.

He married the journalist Frances Edmonds and, in an era when most England players brought their wives out on tour for a week or so, Frances not only covered two entire tours, but also wrote books about them. She even wrote, 'Phil Edmonds the cricketer has a reputation for being awkward and arrogant, mainly because he is awkward and arrogant.'

Edmonds, behind all this, was a great cricketer. An integral part of the brilliant Middlesex side in the 1970s and 1980s, he had a smooth action, although was cursed occasionally by the yips. He was an outstanding fielder, and should have scored far more runs with the bat before he retired in 1987. He was wheeled out when Middlesex were short in 1992 and, after turning up in his Rolls-Royce, still picked up 4–48 against Nottinghamshire. That was his last game, after struggling to walk for a week afterwards.

Having been Chief Executive of Middlesex, as well as a very successful entrepreneur, his business dealings have continued to cause controversy, dabbling in areas such as Sudan and Zimbabwe. To quote the brilliant track by the Super Furry Animals, 'The Man Don't give a Fuck'.

Like him or loathe him, and we – along with the majority of cricket fans – liked him, you cannot dismiss the role he played in England's fine win in India in 1984/85, or the Ashes-winning side in 1986/87, and for that ... Philippe Henri Edmonds, you are a character of cricket.

PHIL TUFNELL - THE BARNET BAMBOOZLER

I first met Tuffers back in 1986. He was playing for Southgate CC, the club who shared a ground with my club, Southgate Adelaide CC, and was already getting a name as a bit of a character. It was from here that many an anecdote concerning the north London left-arm spinner, and one of our favourite characters to have played the game in recent years, arises.

It was around this time, in the mid-1980s, that Tuffers received his first fine as a professional cricketer. The skipper at Southgate at the time was a no-nonsense, gruff-talking Yorkshireman by the name of Mickey Dunn, and it wasn't long before he and the enigmatic Tufnell clashed. Tufnell then lay down on the pitch, refusing to get up and, due to the fact he was wearing a Middlesex second eleven jumper, was relieved of some of his paltry salary – remember, second eleven players at this time were earning around £6,000 per annum, sometimes more, sometimes less.

Tufnell could quite easily have been kicked out of Middlesex at the time – it was him or Jamie Sykes, as together they were a pain and one had to go. Sykes and Tufnell frequented the cells of various police stations more than once during their escapades. Luckily for Tuffers, Phil Edmonds retired, and so a run in the first team followed. Scrapes still came his way, though, and daytimes were filled either with sleep (earning him the nickname of 'the Cat') or wickets, whilst his nights were filled with the warehouse parties or raves we all liked to attend in north London around that summer of love in 1989.

Come the early 1990s, he was now one of the best bowlers in the country, even though Mike Gatting made him go and get a haircut – allegedly sitting in the barbers reading the papers like a parent, to make sure Tufnell got his ponytail removed. Gatting told us, when we interviewed him for my first book *Cricket Banter*, that Tufnell was the scruffiest individual he had ever played with, although closely followed by Mike Brearley. The Cat, meanwhile, bowled Middlesex to the title in 1990, famously giving it the 'large one', as we say in north London, to a bemused Viv Richards after dismissing him down at Cardiff, and was soon selected for an England tour.

It was on this tour to Australia that a few stories began to emerge, such as a threesome in Adelaide that soon turned into a fivesome. It was also on this tour that the famous sledge from the crowd developed: 'Tufnell, lend us your brain, I'm building an idiot'.

The West Indies were soon dismantled back on home soil at the Oval as Tuffers bowled with flight, guile and deceit as they tried to smash him into orbit. He picked up 7 wickets.

It was also around this time that another Tufnell story emerged. Over the years the tabloid press had informed us that he had been through one or two matrimonial problems, and his ex-father-in-law obviously preferred to see the left-arm spin of John Childs in the England side, trying to dislocate Tuffers' shoulder and hitting him with a brick. A high-profile court case followed for Phil, along with his ex-father-in-law, where stories emerged that after an argument that he had locked his ex-wife in a cupboard, and from that day the red tops were all over Tuffers like a cheap suit!

In a completely unrelated incident, the IRA, active at the time on the British mainland, had hijacked a taxi from a firm in Southgate and tried to blow up Downing Street. This was irrelevant to an England cricketer – until Phil popped in to see his mates who ran the taxi company, and it was riddled with paparazzi. Not wishing to be interviewed, or have anything to do with the story in any shape or form, the Cat hid in a cupboard for a few hours until the press had all gone home, although a few hours must have felt like a lifetime when one is absolutely desperate for the toilet.

Further tours followed – he tended to play more abroad than he did at home – and, not being the best of tourists, this was one of numerous strange decisions by the old TCCB throughout the 1990s. The interior redesign of a hotel room one night in Australia followed, as did his removal from a bar in New Zealand as they didn't like the type of smoke emerging from his ciggies, the plumes of which smelt sweet enough that the management reported him to the press for indulging in the art of Jamaican origami.

He became a figure of fun abroad and was pelted with all sorts of missiles from India (where it was mainly fruit) to New Zealand (where it was a cricket bat)! In the West Indies the locals used to throw spliffs at him but, being the conscientious man he is, he collected them all up, no doubt to pass on to the relevant authorities. Or, er … something like that …

Underneath the exterior of the fool being played, however, was a deadly serious bowler who had the ball on a string and gave it some revs. His fielding left a bit to be desired, whilst square leg's toes were often demolished as much as his stumps when he batted, although he did manage to take someone for 67 once. But, by God, could he bowl! He was one of the most attacking spinners we have seen. Dip, flight and turn would be his trademark and, on his day, the slow left-armer was an outstanding bowler.

Eleven wickets against the Aussies in the Test in 1997 on an absolute Bunsen at the Oval followed, and whilst his England career stalled, the wickets kept on coming for Middlesex.

I attended a benefit for him in 1998 at Southgate against a Bunbury XI where Samantha Fox, another illustrious north Londoner, opened the bowling. Her throw – as bowling it was not – barely reached the other end, bouncing as many times as

her mammaries as she ran around the famous Walker Ground. Tuffers proceeded to down copious amounts of the freely flowing rioja that day, and to work his way through the odd cigarette. It was a great day in the sunshine, and I'm sure that Tuffers' head felt like mine the following Monday.

More cigarettes followed, apparently, at Sabina Park when the infamous match was called off with the wicket unfit. 'Scruffnell', as Mike Gatting called him, seeing what happened further up the order to some decent batsmen who were getting hit by balls rearing up from a length, was rumoured to have gone through a packet in just over an hour and a half. Rumours that his arsehole was smoking every time Curtly and Courtney ran in to bowl are unfounded!

Other controversies followed, with stories of various women, missed drugs tests (apparently due to being stung in the eye by a wasp when fielding), and other various matters.

Even when his career ended, it was charismatic. Rather than play for Middlesex, he asked them for a couple of weeks off to go into the jungle for the ITV series, *I'm a Celebrity, Get Me Out of Here*. As it was the cricket season, the club said 'no', so Phil promptly retired. He won the programme, and has since carved out a television career hosting one of the teams on *A Question of Sport*, helping out with *The One Show* (often reporting with a nun), and even getting involved in gardening programmes. Who'd have thought twenty-five years ago that Tuffers would be green-fingered, when he wouldn't have known your *Azalea* from your *Spiraea japonica*? He has also become a decent commentator on *Test Match Special*, offering a view that the common man or bloke down the pub can concur with, as opposed to the highbrow ramblings of Jonathan Agnew.

Now a prolific tweeter, one of the most recent and humorous contacts we had with him was the night of the opening of the Olympics in London 2012. I pointed out to Tuffers via Twitter that he should be opening the ceremony by flicking a discarded Marlboro Light into the cauldron to light the flame. Tuffers found this most amusing, and it was retweeted by numerous members of the twitterati over 500 times, almost crashing my phone and making it vibrate non-stop.

The nation loved his cheeky chappie north London banter, and television's gain is cricket's loss. I genuinely love cricketing characters and Phil Tufnell, whether you love him or hate him, was most certainly one of those. I'm in the former camp, being a cheeky north London chap myself, and so are many more of our followers from around the country.

Philip Clive Roderick Tufnell, we salute you and thank you for some fantastic memories. Not only a fine bowler and a character of the game, but now a true character of our media.

I bloody love Tuffers.

THE BEAUTIFUL ONES

Having recently reread the Nick Hornby classic *High Fidelity*, it seems that men are obsessive about making lists. None more so than here. This made me compile a list of the most graceful stroke makers that I have ever seen. In a way, these guys are just as much characters as some of the bad boys. They would empty bars quickly as people would pay seriously good money to watch them.

Some, like Tom Graveney, Graeme Pollock and Peter May, are before our time but here we look at the prettiest guys to watch over the last forty years. There may have been better bats, but none as good to watch. Here they are, and in no particular order:

DAViD GOWER

The graceful left-hander was my boyhood hero, and whether stroking a cover drive or elegantly flicking off his legs, he would make crowds gasp with some of his stroke play. Like most of the people below, he had a knack of getting out when well-set, but his double hundreds against India in 1979 and Australia in 1985 were a joy to watch. Not many have pulled their first ball in Test cricket for 4, although I believe in his younger years it wasn't just cricket balls that he pulled with regularity …

LAWRENCE ROWE

The Jamaican was described by no less a judge than Michael Holding as 'the best bat I ever saw'. In 1974, when the wickets in the Caribbean were quick and bouncy, not like the slow ones of today, Bob Willis slipped him a quick bouncer in Bridgetown, Barbados. Quick as a flash, Rowe was on to it and hooked it for 6, the ball not going above or below head height before disappearing into a swathe of pissed-up Bajans in the crowd. His career ended in disgrace though, as he led a rebel side to South Africa in 1982.

MARK WAUGH

The complete antithesis of his brother Steve, Mark Waugh was wristy, stylish and fantastic to watch. Part of the great Australian team of the 1990s and early millennium, it was once said that if the Waugh twins were batting in your garden you would pay a fortune to watch Mark, while if twin brother Steve was in, you'd draw the curtains! It just shows what a joy Mark was to watch, as Steve scored a *mere* 54,000 first-class runs! Any bowler who drifted it into middle and leg with Mark was despatched with pure timing, and he was one of the best slip fielders to play the game.

SAEED ANWAR

The Pakistani opener was one of the most exciting opening batsmen of recent years. His flicks and square drives were amazing and his wrists just seemed to extend over the ball. He also had a knack of flicking balls from outside of off-stump over midwicket for 6, making him a complete pain in the arse to bowl to. A committed Muslim, he often saved his best for India, including famously carrying his bat at Eden Gardens in 1999.

MOHAMMAD AZHARUDDIN

If Mark Waugh was the antithesis of Steve, then Azhar's batting was the complete antithesis by way of his facial features! Wristy, delicate and absolutely class off his legs, he was also a fine player of spin. The man who had fangs like Dracula often sucked the life out of the English bowling, and was described by John Woodcock as, 'It's no use asking the English batsmen to play like Azhar. It would be like expecting a greyhound to win the Derby.' Now a politician in India, his career ended in disgrace as match-fixing scandals abounded. A shame, as his career deserved far better.

GREG CHAPPELL

Now a coach, the controversial Chappell scored an absolutely classy hundred against England on debut, in a stand with Ian Redpath. Full of whips through the on-side, allied to a classy cover drive, Greg was an awesome sight to watch in full flow, even for a one-eyed Englishmen like me. A fine captain, the underarm delivery aside, Chappell famously made a protest at Faisalabad in the 1970s at a featherbed pitch, by allowing all eleven Aussies to have a bowl. He also made a citizen's arrest at Lord's, along with Ian Botham, on a MCC member who wasn't being very nice to the umpires. Bless him!

BRIAN LARA

With his high back lift, when this man got in he didn't get out. He played some of his most famous innings under huge pressure, such as his 153 not out against the Aussies in *that* Test match. The only man to score a hundred, a double, a triple, a quadruple and a quintuple century in the history of the game, the darling of the Trini Posse holds the record for the highest score in first-class cricket, as well as Tests. He also came out with one of the best quotes of all time to Mark Ilott in the showers at Chelmsford, when he told the Essex left-armer that he had a clitoris and not a penis, when Ilott found himself showering between two well-endowed West Indian colleagues of Lara's.

ZAHEER ABBAS

The man known as 'Z' or the 'Asian Bradman' was loved universally from Karachi to Clifton, and from Sialkot to Stroud. One of the few players to play wearing glasses, he scored 4 double hundreds in Tests (against England twice in 1971 and 1974) and was a legend down in Bristol for Gloucestershire, scoring 2,000 runs twice for them in his thirteen seasons at the club. Another wristy player, Sunil Gavaskar, once famously told him to 'stop it' in reference to his free scoring. An absolute delight to watch.

DAMiEN MARTYN

A surprising choice, but the Western Australian was worth
the admission fee alone for his back foot driving through
the covers. He kept his head very still, the secret of a great
batsman, and barely looked like he was hitting the ball, just
merely caressing it to the boundary. I have recollections
of watching both him and Mark Waugh bat at Lord's and,
whilst hating every boundary as an Englishman, one could
only admire the stroke play. A fine player, and someone very
underrated in what is, no doubt, the finest-ever side to walk
on to a cricket pitch.

GUNDAPPA ViSWANATH

The 'Mozart of the Willow', Viswanath had a free range
of strokes all around the wicket but only the most foolish
bowler would feed his square cut! He scored a ton as India
famously scored 403 to win in Port of Spain in the fourth
innings in 1976, and was known for his sense of fair play, once
recalling Bob Taylor to the crease. He then became a match
referee, and married Sunil Gavaskar's sister, not that the two
are connected!

CARL HOOPER

Cool Carl Hooper's batting was often erratic, but some of his
shots were just purely 'erotic', as one West Indian fan told me
once. Hooper had amazing footwork, especially against the
spinners, and would often take no less a bowler than Shane
Warne to the cleaners. A reasonable offie too, he is one of only
three players to score hundreds against all eighteen counties
during his stints with Kent and Lancashire. Although having the
middle name 'Llewellyn', there was nothing Welsh about the
Guyanese cool dude.

MiCHAEL VAUGHAN

For a while, in 2003, Michael Vaughan could not put a foot wrong. If the Aussies dropped too short he pulled vigorously, and if they put the ball too far up he would execute his trademark cover drive. He actually made one of the best bowling attacks the world has ever seen look like boys, and did it stylishly and, at times, effortlessly. With his repertoire of strokes, a Michael Vaughan knock was great to watch.

SOURAV GANGULY

Not the most popular man in world cricket, he famously once asked Mike Atherton to carry his kit on arrival in Manchester, but when he was on form, boy, what a player! Through the off-side he was glorious, although not so much off of his legs. His cover, straight and square driving was awesome, though, he had natural timing and a hundred on his debut at Lord's will live in the memory bank.

ALViN KALLiCHARRAN

A touch player, the left-hander and current manager of the Lashings XI was a watchful player. Nineteen seasons at Warwickshire made him a legend in England, and the scorer of 12 Test hundreds in one of the finest teams to ever play the game. He was spotted in the 1980s taking driving lessons in the Welwyn Garden City area of Hertfordshire. I kid you not.

BREARLEY, AMISS AND GAVASKAR – THE PIONEERS

The first cricket box was worn in 1874, but it was not for another 100 years, in the mid-1970s, that cricketers started to protect their second brain – the one in their head!

Well, actually, that is a lie, as players such as Patsy Hendren experimented in the 1930s with wearing numerous caps for protection.

The pioneers of headwear in the 1970s were Mike Brearley, Dennis Amiss and Sunil Gavaskar. The plethora of the super-quick bowlers around the world during this era brought about a train of thought that someone would be killed one day, facing the likes of Andy Roberts or Jeff Thomson.

Before the advent of the helmet, batsmen tended to sway as opposed to ducking, as they could keep their eye on the ball for longer. According to my sources, who include ex-Middlesex professionals who shared a dressing room with him, Brearley was concerned that if he was hit in the temple facing the likes of Jeff Thomson at 99mph, he would be heading upstairs to St Peter's gates, as opposed to leaving peacefully out of the Grace Gates.

The Middlesex physio at the time was a chap called Johnny Miller, who was almost blind and would have to be led on to the pitch by the twelfth man after getting lost in the Long Room on numerous occasions! John tinkered with the idea of using mouldable, hard plastic as protection for wicketkeepers' fingers, arm guards, short-leg shin pads, and the like, and Brearley asked him to design him a form of head protection. Many a skull cap has been worn around the north London area, but none as famous as the head apparel worn by the best England captain of all time.

Richard Ellis tells us that initially Brearley was ridiculed by not only his own teammates but by the oppo, particularly the quicks who would target said cap. Mike Selvey, another to play in the same side, and now the chief cricket correspondent of the *Guardian*, told us that Brearley actually cut his own hair and glued it on the side, trying to hide the fact he was wearing one in these masculine times!

Another to utilise the skull cap was the Indian opening batsman Sunil Gavaskar, who played over here for Somerset. Gavaskar was a man who did not drink, did not smoke and did not gamble, although Ian Botham once heard him say, 'Oh my goodness!' Not used to the bounce of wickets away from his native Bombay, which barely rose above shin height, there was no hiding under a cap for Sunil as the plethora of overseas quicks in the county game targeted the diminutive Indian.

This evolved, and Dennis Amiss started to wear the kind of full-on helmet that Evel Knievel would have worn as he attempted to jump London buses. Graeme Yallop then became one of the first people to wear one regularly in a Test match in 1978, and the lid with the Perspex visor soon became de rigueur for the likes of Geoffrey Boycott.

Ellis recalled that he made his debut for Middlesex as twelfth man when Keith Tomlins was wearing said Perspex visor at short leg before copping a full-blooded pull between the gap. As the unfortunate Tomlins was led bleeding profusely from the field, Ellis, being the team youngster was thrown the lid and told to get in there. When he put it on, the visor was covered in more blood than that produced by your average Saturday night out in Glasgow, before the apologetic Brearley got it cleaned. A few years later, as protection evolved, Ellis was one of numerous batsmen on the circuit to get hit on the head by the hostile Sylvester Clarke on a quick deck at the Oval. This time it hit him in the metal grille and the only thing damaged was the ball.

Other batsmen to have had their lives saved by the helmet include Andy Lloyd for England, who was pinned on his Test debut by Malcolm Marshall in 1984, and still spent three days in hospital. Without headwear, he would have been using a coffin for a far different purpose than carrying his kit around! Bruce Yardley was another to get hit badly, fielding at short leg in a game in Australia.

To see close fielders and now even wicketkeepers wearing a lid whilst standing up has become the norm, and as cricket evolves, and pioneers in this field such as the Bristol-based Ayrtek lead the way, helmets have become much safer. You even have a button to pump the helmet up so that the lid fits the head, whilst anything that hits it is designed to deflect more than Monty Panesar in a press conference. Like cycling, with the wind designed to move around the helmet, technology has made the cricket helmet far safer. The likes of James Taylor or Michael Carberry with their Bradley Wiggins-style lids were ridiculed at first, as people like Brearley and Amiss were a generation before, but one thing is for certain – the cricket helmet is here to stay.

The tragic death of the Australian batsman Phillip Hughes in November 2014 should be a reminder that these guys and their feats should be applauded and that without their pioneerism other cricketers may have suffered the sad same fate. Hughes' injury was a freak occurrence, and a horrendous time for the game in general. Hopefully the initial steps put in place by Brearley, Gavaskar and Amiss will save lives in the future. A cricket ball hurts, and intimidation is part of the game. Professional sport is no tea party, but the loss of Hughes should mean that safety steps within the game of cricket have to keep evolving. There would be no better legacy for a fine player and man.

These characters were pioneers of the modern game.

MAGICAL MICHAEL

Watching Alastair Cook in India in December 2011 was a joy to behold. He had driven more Indians that winter than your average tuk-tuk taxi operator, and without a doubt he was in the form of his life. As I wrote this on a Saturday night during that cold, dark winter, Michael Vaughan suddenly sprang to mind. Not because we were seeing the twinkle toed ex-England skipper on our screens during *Strictly Come Dancing* at this time, but because he was the last Englishman to offer such resistance abroad before Cook and, judging by the form of our lot out in Australia, none since.

Vaughan was one of my favourite English cricketers of recent years. On the surface a charming and pleasant man, but no doubt one with as much inner steel as befits a man from Sheffield. It was a term that coach Duncan Fletcher would elegantly term 'dogfuck', describing in blunt Southern African terminology the inner desire needed to be an elite sportsman. One of the first Yorkshiremen born outside the county to play for the White Rose (no less a man than Sachin Tendulkar was the first), Vaughan was an elegant player, described by some as a modern-day Peter May. Now I might be an old bastard, but even I didn't see May bat, so cannot comment, but to watch him go head to head with one of the finest Australian attacks conjured up some jingoistic Dunkirk spirit.

He first came into the England side in Johannesburg in light that made Joey Essex look bright. England were 2–4 and Shaun Pollock was seaming it everywhere, whilst Allan Donald bowled a seriously rapid spell. Vaughan stood firm and despite making only 30-odd, you could sense that he had something very special about him.

He was also only the second Englishman to be given out handled the ball. As the ball trickled backwards towards his stumps, Vaughan instinctively moved it with his hand resulting in this rare form of dismissal. Maybe he should have emulated the footwork, instead of the handwork, of Diego Maradona more when he had to do the Argentine tango on *Strictly*? Saying that, he has emulated the show's host Sir Bruce Forsyth by having a hair weave, with Vaughan's coming via the Advanced Hair Studio, whilst Brucie's came from Allied Carpets. Unlike the BCCI, these two have embraced the DRS – Dodgy Rugs and Syrups!

Vaughan, however, continued to play his cards right during his early England career, and 2002 brought him a plethora of runs. Sri Lanka and India were put to the sword. He did start with a duck against the Indians, but after having a chat with the host of *Strictly Come Dancing,* who told him that 'you get nothing for a pair in this game', he decided to ton-up in the second knock. Scores of 195 and 197 in this series were merely the aperitif before arriving in Australia.

Australia at this time were simply awesome. Vaughan, however, thought that too many English players talked up the likes of Warne and McGrath, and decided to front-up and take it to them, having been advised to in the previous summer by Sachin Tendulkar. In the second Test at Adelaide he got a cheeky 145, before a delightful 177 at Melbourne. Anything short was pulled, whilst anything too full was caressed to the cover boundary. It was quite simply stunning to watch. Even The Middle Stump interviewee Australian paceman Jason Gillespie breaking his shoulder didn't stop Vaughan, and a 183 at Sydney was only stopped by a decision that was so poor it was akin to the executives at Decca Records who turned down the Beatles.

On his return to England the runs didn't stop, and 156 versus South Africa gave him the chance to skipper England in the wake of Nasser's resignation. Under Vaughan we became the first side to win away in the West Indies since 1968, thanks to Steve Harmison whose 7–12 in Jamaica, along with the umbrella field set by the skipper, will live in the memory bank.

Back home, New Zealand and the Windies again were despatched, England victorious in all 7 Tests, before an away win in South Africa. Come 2005, and that bit of 'dogfuck' again came to the surface. England were aggressive and in Australian faces. Simon Jones set the scene by hurling the ball back at Matt Hayden in a One Day game, and when Harmy pinned Ponting at Lord's, cutting his cheek open, no one asked him if he was ok. England, under Vaughan, had finally hardened up. With this sort of track record, and, no wonder he was invited on to the dancing show. Would he now be known universally as 'Viagra Vaughan'?

A rather fortunate 166 against the Aussies at Old Trafford followed, before England finally sealed the Ashes at the Oval for the first time since 1986. He was as passionate about England as he is about his beloved Sheffield Wednesday, and Owls fan Vaughan was rightly awarded an OBE for his efforts.

Three years later, and minus most of his knee cartilage, Vaughan resigned in tears at Edgbaston. I have to admit I cried with him watching it. Funny isn't it, how this does it to you when it is an Englishman, but I howled with laughter as a kid when Kim Hughes did the same whilst he was the Australian captain?

Now a respected journalist, he is part of the *Test Match Special* and the Channel 5 team, and his award-winning radio programme about 'Depression in Cricket' was extremely thought provoking. He continues to be outspoken about match-fixing and one famous headline during the Pakistan series said, 'Vaughan wants Butt Legal Action'. Rumours that our website, The Middle Stump, was going to be forthcoming with a copy of a certain DVD cannot be confirmed. He has become a celebrity who has transcended the game, and I for one look forward to him being on our television screens in the future, as I look forward to Alastair Cook churning out hundreds in the present.

Michael, thanks for the memories.

DAVID SMITH – THE BALHAM BRUISER

David Smith was a character who played county cricket for over twenty years between 1973 and 1994. Born in Balham in south London, when it was a very different place from what it is now – a hard, working-class south London suburb, as opposed to the trendy Clapham overspill. He went to school in Battersea, just a Monte Lynch six-hit away from the Oval, where he started his career.

Smith was the enforcer of the Surrey side, a hard man, and was sacked and reinstated three times in Kennington. One recollection I have is of about twenty-five of us going to watch Surrey versus Hertfordshire at the Oval in the NatWest Trophy first round in June 1987. It was my birthday, plus a few of the lads knew some of the Herts boys, so we went down for a day out. The game was only fifteen or twenty overs off when the following incident occurred. One of our number was overly loud about a number of the Surrey players, such as describing Graham Clinton as looking like the character Fu Manchu, and mentioning that Jack Richards had lost his England place as he wasn't good enough.

Within a couple of minutes the gargantuan figure of David Smith had appeared, and basically offered any one of us a fight behind the pavilion after the game. Naturally, the language he used cannot be repeated in such a high-class publication such as this, but let's just say he kept referring to us as a 'vulgar form of the female genitalia' (as the *Oxford English Dictionary* describes that word). The game was held up for a good five minutes as Smith stood there offering us his form of south London wit. Shakespeare he was most certainly not. And all this at around half eleven in the morning, when everyone was stone cold sober.

A young Alec Stewart was fielding on the boundary and told us 'Not to worry about Smudger, he just gets a bit excitable', before disappearing back into the old pavilion at the Oval, Smith's preferred venue of choice for a punch-up.

Excitable wasn't the phrase I would use after the game, as we went on the pitch for the 'Man of the Match' award, which you could do back in those day without fear of getting banned from sports events or contravening any laws. The only fear that I had soon came to haunt me as I was shoved in the chest by this hulking, moustachioed left-hander. The 6ft 4in Smith, along with his terrier Jack Richards hiding behind him, decided they would like to continue the argument. I wouldn't mind but the initial row was nothing to do with me, yet here I was about to get 'chinned', as they say in this part of the world, by a bloke who was seriously huge. We left it before it got out of hand, but fair play to the 'Balham Bruiser', who was willing to fight twenty-five blokes on his own!

Paul Nixon tells another story, in his book *Keeping Quiet*, about Smith when he was a youngster, winding down his career at Sussex. Nico basically chatted him out and as he went off, the south Londoner gave him a look which wasn't a friendly stare. With other characters you wouldn't even think about it once he had been dismissed, but Smith was a different kettle of fish. When the Leicester stumper's teammates told him to watch out as he had gone too far, he started to worry, and then even more so when our friend from Balham punched a hole in the dressing room door.

In the car park after the day's play, Smith was there waiting, and Nixon had no choice but to walk past him. Smith pulled him up, and the wicketkeeper thought 'Just hit me and get it over with'. Smith then went into a speech about how he had got under his skin, and Nico was expecting to get battered by the huge Smith. Unbelievably Smith half-smiled, saying 'I shouldn't have let you do that', and Nixon had got away with it. Maybe, just maybe, the Battersea behemoth was maturing!

There's no doubt Smith could play, though. A tall left-hander, he was one of the best players of fast bowling in the country and was taken on two tours of the West Indies in 1986 and 1990. Various Surrey players were brought into the England team during the 1980s, and Smith had earned his place in the national side through sheer weight of runs. Others, such as Monte Lynch, had been picked because Mike Gatting thought someone said lunch, so the old story goes.

A broken thumb curtailed one of the Tests, but he was top scorer in his second Test match, before a bad back ruined this one for him. He was then flown out as cover for Graham Gooch when he was victim to one of the many broken bones around the Caribbean at that time.

Spells at Worcestershire and Sussex came in between his Oval sackings, and a brilliant 124 in the 1994 NatWest final for Sussex was still not enough, as they lost despite scoring over 300. He then went into coaching for Sussex, but God knows what he is doing now.

Cricket doesn't make too many characters like David Smith.

DEREK RANDALL - THE CLOWN PRINCE

Derek William Randall was a legend, and one of the most popular players to ever wear the English shirt. Known as 'Rags', or 'Arkle' (named after the famous racehorse) he was loved and adored by the cricketing public. However, like most clowns, there was a touch of sadness as well as madness about the Nottinghamshire man, along with some moments of sheer genius. Here we look back on the career of the man, described as a loveable lunatic.

Having started his career in the Nottinghamshire leagues, he was soon noticed as a good local player and became a regular fixture at Trent Bridge, after making his debut in 1972. He came to prominence in the Centenary Test of 1977 in Australia, making a brilliant 174, hooking off the end of his nose in the days when helmets were not worn. One bouncer from Dennis Lillee in that match didn't miss his nose by that much, causing Arkle to doff his cap to Lillee. Legend has it that Derek said, 'No point hitting me there mate, there is nothing in it'. Let's just say the man from Perth didn't see the amusing side to the Retford rhetoric!

Randall then left the dressing rooms via the wrong gate and found himself in the Royal Enclosure face to face with the Queen.

Later that year Randall, having taken the catch that won the Ashes, produced cartwheel upon cartwheel on the turf, delighting the crowd. Randall was involved in numerous run outs throughout his career, and not all of them for the opposition. He and Geoff Boycott were an absolute nightmare and it was a classic case of the tortoise and the hare. He was a nightmare for Gordon Greenidge too, running him out brilliantly at the start of the 1979 World Cup final at Lord's. Randall on one side of the wicket and Gower on the other were part of the first era of brilliant fielders that the One Day game had produced.

Part of Randall's success in this aspect was that he would drop off 30 or 40 metres, and with his reputation for dozing off, the batsman would think they could take a cheeky single to him. However, Rags would sprint in – sometimes quicker than the bowler – to make himself in the right position, fooling the batsman.

Mike Gatting told us recently, as part of an interview in our first book *Cricket Banter*, that Randall would hurl the ball into the air and practise catching it behind his back. Gatt said, 'If you or I tried that, we'd end up with concussion, but he would catch it nearly every time with his hands behind his back. Amazing.'

Another story regarding Randall was that he regularly used to leave taps on in hotel rooms, flooding the place, and has been described by many who played with him as 'away with the fairies'.

However, you don't score nearly 30,000 first-class runs by being a complete looney. His average was actually decent for England lower down the order, but he was in and out more times than your average night with Shane Warne and a promotions girl, whilst in the order, he was up and down like Monica Lewinsky in an office in the White House back in the '90s – allegedly!

Rags nearly won the 1985 NatWest final for his beloved Notts. Needing 18 off the last over, Randall hit the first five balls for 16, before being caught off of the last ball. He turned out in the competition a few years later for Suffolk at the age of 49, no doubt still hooking off his nose.

The last Randall story that sticks in the memory is of him going back to his hotel room once on England duty whilst playing at Lord's. Having tried the key in Room 128 at one of the big ones down the road from the Grace Gates, he found the key wouldn't turn. He looked at the fob and checked that it was indeed Room 128 he was staying at. Having tried it for nearly an hour, Randall called the security guard, only for the gentleman to inform him that he had entered the wrong hotel and this was where he normally stayed with Nottinghamshire! England were actually staying in the hotel next door.

The game of cricket certainly misses characters like Derek William Randall. Those people we have spoken to up in Nottinghamshire most certainly do.

'OPPO SPEAK' - A DYING ART?

The following article isn't about the characters of cricket per se, but more about the environment that has produced virtually every character that this wonderful game has given us. This is about the dying art of teams having a drink with each other after the game, and no doubt many of you reading this will completely agree with me. This was where I met many of the characters who formed my love for the game, and too many of the youngsters these days will never get to know some of the amazing characters we learned our stories from throughout north London cricket.

Players can learn a hell of a lot by indulging in what we call 'oppo speak', and this is where the characters of the game were found every Saturday night in the summer months, at every cricket club in the country. The term derived from speaking with the opposition, or as we colloquially termed them, 'the oppo'. Getting the lowdown on your forthcoming teams in the next few weeks' fixtures would help no end, as well as putting vital funds behind club bars. Taking a jug around the oppo was part of what the youngsters used to have to do in the bar, and was a great learning curve for us. We hope this article doesn't make too many of the youngsters today choke on their energy drink:

> Cricket is not about playing the game, having half a lemonade and pissing off home, it's about having a few pints of beer and talking to the opposition about the game.

That quote was given to us by Percy Geypersad, a very well-known Indian cricketer and umpire on the north London circuit who was a great ambassador for his club, Calthorpe CC.

When I was a 15 year old in the mid-1980s, one thing that was drummed into me was that you did not go home straight after the game. You waited at least until the opposition had left your bar and you went out of your way to discuss the game with the opposition. I remember one away game in particular when, along with some older stalwarts, I gatecrashed a corporate barbecue. When I asked if I could get a lift home on this particular Sunday evening I was asked, 'what are you gonna do at home?' as the older guys looked at me in a strange manner, aghast at the thought that someone would go home straight after a day's play. Often at the end of a hammering in a friendly game you would be instructed by the skipper that you had to 'drink the fixture back'.

In those days, cricketers/characters on the circuit were far better known. When you were to play any side, you looked out for those characters, and they looked out for you. I've lost count of the number of times that I arrived at an opposition ground and was greeted with 'alright boys, where's your such and such?' with reference to one of the characters within your own team who no doubt had shared a beer or two with said gentlemen in the previous season's fixture. I think it is fair to say that we had plenty of those said characters, and both myself and John Thorp, who has helped me write this book, became integral members of the characters of the local circuit.

That's because we were of the generation when 'oppo speak' was a major part of the game. We spent many a long evening speaking cricket and anything else that came to mind with opposition players over many years. That was also, in many ways, the university of banter; it set you up as a social character in wider life, learning how to mix with people from all backgrounds and cultures, and mixing with adults as kids.

We were sometimes marvelled at for knowing every player from every team. We were also sometimes criticised for being too matey with the players we had faced up against, and then drank with in the bar for many years, by our own teammates, but to my mind that was a big part of the game and was of financial importance to the stability of the club. Many times, members of the opposition would stay on as they knew the home players, and were engaged by them, often putting vital funds behind a home bar.

Young players can also learn important lessons during periods of 'oppo speak'. I remember one particular night when our club, Southgate Adelaide, had claimed their most famous ever scalp, Dunstable, in a game heavily affected by rain. Their skipper, the Bedfordshire captain Dave Mercer and opening bowler Bob 'who ploughed through my defences' Ploughman, stayed in our bar until about 10 p.m., talking cricket with us youngsters. These were decent minor counties players and no doubt we all learnt something. Okay, we may have continued making the same mistakes week in and out, but we soaked up the gems they gave us that night.

In the last few years in club cricket, I am dismayed at how the art of 'oppo speak' has fallen away. Either the bar clears out very quickly, with the opposition basically ignored and the home players departing almost as quickly as them, or the home players crowd round the fruit machine, pool table or dart board, with no cross-team discussion about the day's cricket sparking off. Even now, as vice president when I occasionally attend games and pop back into old cricketing haunts to which I ventured many years ago, the young lads look to the old lags to spark off any sort of bar room atmosphere. Where are the young guns, full of life and lager, giving it large, exchanging stories and giggles with the opposition and teammates, or even having races drinking pints down-in-one, upside down on their heads as we did back in our day?

Is it a consequence of the Internet and iPhone generation? On football fans' blog sites, the old lags who actually manage to drag their armchairs through the turnstiles often find themselves in conflict with the Xbox generation. Their ideal of social interaction through football is spending their weekends flicking through the Internet for highlights in between gaming sessions, and then making daft comments on message boards. Not exactly the same as getting hammered with yer mates and actually going to the games, home and away, is it?

A lot of communication these days is electronic rather than face-to-face, but club cricket, particularly Sunday games, was friendly stuff that thrived in the 1980s and 1990s. The game used to be about the big characters. The drinking and social aspect of clubs and players was a big part of who you sorted out for a Sunday fixture. It also played a part in selection, as I remember one of the reasons being given for the selection of a player being as 'he's got a car and he talks to the opposition'.

Often having been cited as having 'verbal diarrhoea', I am at one end of the spectrum, but surely there is a happy middle ground between the likes of the authors of this work and the type of monosyllabic youngsters you see at cricket clubs today, glowering at the opposition on the field, ignoring them in the bar and staring at their iPhone, while sipping a Lucozade?

There has to be, if club cricket below the elite level is going to survive.

EDDIE HEMMINGS - YOU COST ME A FIVER!

After writing about the more rotund players around the circuit, we at The Middle Stump asked people on Twitter a couple of years ago who would be in their 'Cricket Fatties' XI. The same names kept coming back to us, but one in particular, and that was a certain Edward Ernest Hemmings, with Ed Giddins telling us that he could have modelled for Millets if he had lost 7 stone.

Eddie made his introduction to Test cricket quite late, at the tender age of 33, but I didn't actually realise that he had been a seam bowler early in his career. Eddie first toured Australia in 1982, edging out Vic Marks as the other spinner. It was on this tour that my favourite Eddie story arose.

Eddie was now a Nottinghamshire player, but was walking back to his hotel with ex-teammate from Warwickshire, Gladstone Small. Eddie was approached by an expat Brummie, and this gentleman was wanting to talk all things Birmingham, Warwickshire and cricket with the moustachioed offie. After a million questions, the gentleman asked about Gladstone Small, and asked Eddie what he was like. Polite as ever, Eddie remarked that this was indeed Gladstone walking with him and would he like to meet him? The bloke took one look at the hunchback walking with Hemmings, and said in the broadest Brummie accent, 'Well there's no need to take the piss, Eddie. I was only trying to be nice', and walked off!

It was also on this tour that some Australian comedian let a live pig loose in the outfield. On one side he had sprayed the word 'Eddie' and on the other, 'Botham'. This was in reference to the portly shape of some of the England players at the time. Graeme Fowler was in a car with him on the way home, with others including Allan Lamb. Hemmings was never the quickest behind the wheel, and none of the England players dared mention the pig incident, until Fowler piped up with, 'C'mon Eddie, put your trotter down'. To say he wasn't amused would be an understatement, and only the intervention of Lamb and the fact that they were on a freeway stopped Hemmings from making Fowler walk home.

Eddie has actually cost me money. In 1990, India played at Lord's in a game famous for Graham Gooch's 333. With 24 runs needed to avoid the follow on and 1 wicket left, my mate bet me a fiver they would make it. I quite happily accepted the bet, as I knew their No. 11, Hirwani, barely knew which end of the bat to hold. However, thanks to Eddie, the blue piece of paper was out of my hands four balls later, as Kapil Dev hit him for 4 sixes to avoid the follow on. Good job he did as well, as Hirwani was lbw to Gus Fraser the very first ball of the next over!

In true Eddie style, he claimed that England wouldn't have won the game if India had followed on, as the bowlers were all tired, and England batting gave them a chance to put their feet up. He also dropped a certain 16 year old in the second knock, who scored the first of his 100 International centuries, one Sachin Tendulkar.

Whilst researching Eddie, a story comes from the Nottinghamshire league of one of our friends on Twitter, now living in France. Having been smashed for a couple of sixes, Hemmings threw a massive wobbly apparently, although was found afterwards taking solace in the cakes at the tea interval.

However, Eddie wasn't just a figure of fun. He was one of the tightest bowlers around in One Day cricket, and he could bat as well. He scored 95 as a nightwatchman against the Aussies once, and I also remember him having plenty of words to say to Geoff 'Henry' Lawson in a losing cause in 1989. Those from Robin Hood's county will no doubt remember him slapping the economical John Lever for 4 in a One Day final as well, to win the game off the last ball.

The man himself retired at the age of 46 after a little stint with Sussex, and now runs a shop in Lincolnshire. His niece, Beth Morgan, plays for the England ladies' team. Characters like Eddie are sadly now all too rare in the game, and he gave us plenty of great moments in the 1980s.

Eddie Hemmings, you are most definitely one of the characters of this wonderful game.

'RUPERT' ROEBUCK

Peter Roebuck was a bloke who seriously polarised opinions. People were either generally a fan of one of the finest cricket writers ever to walk this earth, or had a vile revulsion towards him in a way a man with a nut allergy would handle a packet of dry roasted.

It is not my intention to cane Roebuck in this article, although cane would be an operative word, seeing as the ex-Somerset man had a penchant for punishing young overseas players who would be guests in his house.

His career started at Millfield School and, after a stint at Cambridge University where he studied law, he soon played for the county in which Millfield is located. A stoic batsman, he was the snail in their middle order compared to the gazelles of Richards, Botham or even Peter 'Dasher' Denning.

He was known to all and sundry as 'Rupert', after Keith Fletcher called him that shortly after making his debut in 1974, when a fellow Somerset player had told the Essex man that was his name. Fletcher mistakenly called him 'Rupert' all day, much to the amusement of the cider men and after that the name stuck.

Bespectacled and often lank-haired, looking like the school swot (or, if anyone remembers the comic *Viz*, the character Mr Logic), Roebuck was part of the famous Somerset side that won the county's first piece of silverware in 1979, and would collect numerous titles after that, albeit never the county championship.

However, it was in 1986 that he really came to the forefront of controversy, being the man who campaigned to sack Vivian Richards and Joel Garner. This was on the basis that the West Indians were past their sell-by date, and the Somerset members, having been through a famine that followed the feast of previous seasons, voted with Roebuck in an acrimonious meeting in Shepton Mallet.

The good ship Botham resigned shortly after, loyal as ever in backing up his West Indian teammates, and sailed up the River Severn to Worcester, with Martin Crowe becoming the overseas player. This part of the world hadn't seen such civil uprising since Alfred the Great burnt the cakes, but Roebuck had a habit of rubbing people up the wrong way, metaphorically speaking.

One of the *Wisden* cricketers of the year in 1988, Roebuck eventually played minor counties cricket for Devon before becoming estranged from England as Australian citizenship was bestowed upon him. He became distant from the country of his birth; so much so that he was affronted by being called a 'Pom' once, whilst in Sydney. His pen became fairly vitriolic towards the English team, although he was always a stickler for fair play, the lack of walking by batsmen being a particular target of his vitriol. He once said of Justin Langer, 'When Justin Langer finds his off stump akimbo he leaves the crease only after asking the Met. Office whether any earthquakes have been recorded in the region. In any case, he never edges the ball. It's just that his bat handle keeps breaking.'

Roebuck became one of the finest journalists in the world, his column in the *Sydney Age* a cornucopia of erudite cricketing opinions, but stories would abound about his own private life. A conviction in 1999 for caning the buttocks of three South African 19-year-old players who stayed in his house was scandalous, although one of the young gentlemen went on record to say he didn't mind being caned, but it was when Roebuck wanted to inspect the marks that the alarm bells started to ring.

It was also a 20-something cricketer from Zimbabwe who told police he had been groomed by Roebuck, leading police to visit him on the sixth floor of the Southern Sun Hotel in Cape Town. On 12 November 2011 at 9.15 p.m. Roebuck requested to phone a friend to get him a lawyer before, tragically, jumping to his death from the sixth floor. He was killed instantly due to a serious head trauma.

Even in death, Roebuck polarised opinion. Although there were those who despised the man, on the other hand, many mourned one of the finest journalists that the cricketing world has seen. Not many people sat on the fence when it came to him, and like him or loathe him (for not many people were ambivalent to his ways), there is no doubt that he was one of the characters of the game of recent years.

VIOLENT VERMEULEN?

Mark Vermeulen was a schoolboy protégé in his native Zimbabwe. A fine back foot opening batsman, his main run-scoring shots were the cut, the pull and the hook, although he also had a decent cover drive. He had all the talent in the world, but temperamentally he also gave the world's press more than enough highlights to make him an integral part of this book.

His disciplinary problems started in school cricket back in 1996. Representing the privileged Prince Edwards in Harare, Mark was so disgruntled with an lbw decision from one of the umpires that he picked up the stumps and locked himself in the dressing room. With the game being abandoned due to lack of facilities, he was suspended from his school team.

After making his Test debut, more disciplinary problems came to the surface. The tour to England in 2003 was awash with tantrums and tears, and Vermeulen's behaviour was about as stable as that of Zimbabwean leader Robert Mugabe at the time. Fined during a warm-up game at Hove for refusing to stop a ball on the grounds that it was too cold, he then refused to travel with the rest of the team after becoming only the thirteenth player in history to be out twice in one day for a pair at Lord's, before being sent home.

In 2004 he was hit by a sickening delivery to the head by Irfan Pathan in a VB Series match in Australia, and had to have surgery to reconstruct a fractured skull. The doctor who performed the surgery warned the Zimbabwean that further blows to the head could be life threatening, yet he was back batting just four months later. It was after this that his behaviour started to become even more erratic.

A huge dip in form followed, along with the break-up with his fiancée, but 2006 seemed to be his *annus horribilis*. Playing for Werneth CC who are based in Oldham, Lancashire, in a Central Lancashire league match he bowled an over which went for quite a few in a game versus Ashton. Barracked by a wag in the crowd, Vermeulen hurled the ball at the said Lancastrian loudmouth with all of the accuracy he had displayed a few moments before in his wayward over. Having just missed a small child, he carried on by then picking up a boundary marker and hurling that into the crowd. Not just any old boundary marker, I hasten to add, but one of those that you spear into the ground spike end first. Maybe the schoolboy javelin champion was re-enacting his youth on the field, minus the track of the track-and-field based sport? Wrestled to the ground by his own supporters from Werneth, the 6ft 4in Vermeulen was given a ten-year ban, later reduced to three, for going against the spirit of the game. Funny that.

Upon returning to Harare, he was then left out of his country's thirty-man squad and the pressure cooker of his mind blew once more. Not content with trying to break into the house of Robert Mugabe to plead his case for inclusion in the squad, a dangerous enough pastime in itself, this time he really inflamed the situation by attempting to burn down the Zimbabwe cricket headquarters. Just merely catching the curtains before being spotted, he drove the following night to the academy 5 miles away, completing the job properly as the whole lot went up. In such an impoverished country, all of their technical equipment and facilities followed in a similar vein to Mark's career prospects.

Looking at a minimum of twenty-five years inside, a Harare jail would have been a harsh environment for a rich kid who was the son of a dentist. He was cleared on the grounds of being mentally ill, and promised to pay back the damage that he had caused. This came to £47,000, although in this country of rising inflation, rumour has it that he had only caused £1,500 worth of damage! Vermeulen returned to the Zimbabwe team at the age of 30, and is still playing to this day.

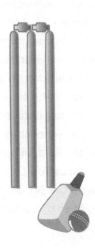

Having taken tablets for epilepsy, we can only pray that he never returns as a winning member of an IPL team with all of the flashing lights that goes with that ceremony. If so, watch out.

THE FOX

Graeme Fowler was one of my heroes growing up. My co-host at The Middle Stump, Liam, still tells me I was squealing like a 12-year-old girl interviewing him. As someone who admired his shots and his athletic fielding, I was nervous about interviewing the Accringtonian last year, but found him to be one of the friendliest, funniest people that we have encountered, and what followed was one of the more amusing conversations I have had.

Fowler was born in the Lancashire town in 1957 and, after several successful seasons in the Lancashire league, along with being a prolific scorer for Durham University, he became a professional at Old Trafford in 1979. A reserve wicketkeeper in his younger days, Fowler broke into the side in the late 1970s and by 1982 he had been picked for England.

It was his skipper Bob Willis who first introduced him to the team as 'Foxy Fowler' and, hearing the cries of 'well chased Fox' or 'good work Foxy' made Fowler think, 'who the fuck are they talking to?', before suddenly realising they were talking to him. A century followed against New Zealand, before becoming the star of the English campaign in the 1983 World Cup. He then scored one of the fastest hundreds of all time for Lancashire as he milked the short boundary and the declaration bowling of none other than David Gower, quicker than a nurse milks your prostate gland.

A hundred against the West Indies at Lord's in 1984 followed, against arguably the best side of all time. It was during this game that Fowler had his box broken by Joel Garner ten minutes before lunch, and he allowed his teammates to visit Nancy's famous dining room before taking the shattered remnants out bit by bit, checking that his crown jewels were still intact. A double hundred followed, on the winter tour of India as he compiled 201, where the Fox had the highest score ever by an Englishman for about an hour, before Mike Gatting feasted on the Indian attack. This was the tour that nearly never happened after Indian Prime Minister Indira Gandhi was assassinated within hours of England arriving, and the English High Commissioner was murdered several days later in the riot-torn country. With security beefed up, Fowler was allegedly the favourite to get shot by a sniper in the crowd, on the basis that the opener would be the first one out there, as gallows humour enveloped the England dressing room.

Amazingly Fowler was dropped a Test later, and never played for England again. His form had dipped horrendously due to a neck injury that had occurred in the late 1970s. A car crash in 1979 had caused a broken leg, but X-rays had never picked up that he had also broken his neck and he had played for years with this injury. By 1985 this problem got so bad that he couldn't turn his head or get his hands through the ball, an injury which tends to affect your performance as an opening batsman. Not many can say they scored a double hundred in their penultimate Test match.

His form slumped, and his book *Fox on the Run*, which is a diary of this time, can make painful reading to those who have been out of form. One anecdote that arises from this period of misfortune still makes me chuckle to this day. The opener was really out of nick but had battled through the last hour of a county game, and with one ball to go, his mate, the Derbyshire off-spinner Geoff Miller, had deliberately thrown a wide one outside off-stump, in the hope that Foxy would leave it and they could all come back in the morning and start again. Fowler unfortunately followed it, nicking off to the keeper. Furious with himself, he didn't even bother getting changed out of his whites and got in his car, screeching out of the Old Trafford car park. Still fuming when he arrived home, it was only when he looked down he realised that he still had his pads on.

Still a joker, Fowler commented recently that *Fox on the Run* is a book of two halves. The first is the period of England success, and the second is a deep and dark look into someone struggling to do their job as well as they can. One follower asked about the book recently, and he quipped, 'It's a bit sad, but don't worry, I don't die or anything like that.'

Loved by Lancastrians, the Inspiral Carpets guitarist Graham Lambert says he was one of his favourite bats. He left the county in 1992, before finishing his career at Durham, where he still lives to this day, having devised and created the University Centre of Excellence in the famous city. He has coached many of today's current professionals as well as the likes of Andrew Strauss.

Now a part-time commentator on *Test Match Sofa* (or *Guerilla Cricket* as it is now called) where I met him, Fowler has raised awareness of depression, having suffered with the condition himself for long periods of his life. The work he does in this arena, whilst hugely important and discussing a delicate and vital subject, is still done with good humour and grace. For this work alone he deserves credit.

One of the game's characters, it has been a pleasure to have got to know Foxy in recent years, discussing a diverse range of subjects like why cricketers get piles or Frank Hayes' drinking ability. Long may his tweeting continue …

CRICKETING CRIMINALS

As England prepared to combat the descendants of colonial criminals in Australia, much was made of their famous, or now shall we say infamous, menu, which was leaked to expose England's dietary habits. However, for this bunch below, porridge is the normal fare. These characters of cricket have all had a brush with the law and know that bail is not just something that sits on top of the stumps. A pre-match stretch to this lot is nothing new, and hitting one out of the middle of the screws would be an uncomfortable night in! Here we look at a few of the chaps who have spent a bit of time in a cell, with cricketing connections:

SALMAN BUTT, MOHAMMAD ASIF AND MOHAMMAD AMIR

The Pakistani trio all received a stretch in recent years for spot-fixing, a process where they deliberately bowled no-balls for financial gain. Rumours that the two older players had a defence that went along the lines of 'I put it to you, Mr Butt, that you spot-fixed?' He replied 'As if', then his partner was asked the same question and stammered, 'But … ' leading to guilty verdicts. Either that or it was fairly obvious when Amir suddenly bowled a 2ft no-ball at Lord's that something naughty was going on. Skipper Butt, got thirty months, Asif twelve months and Amir got six months' bird in a Young Offender's Institution.

MERVYN WESTFIELD

The Essex quick got dragged into match-fixing, along with teammate Danish Kaneria, and was silly enough to show his teammates the money. Kaneria had to go for 12 off an over, which he achieved, and Westfield got four months for his troubles. Rumours that many a bowler of the past is now seriously worried they might find themselves on similar charges, having been slapped to the boundary regularly, are unfounded. How Kaneria walked scot-free is a mystery and Westfield, who had a rough time in prison, is now hoping to rebuild his life.

Westfield's club Wanstead CC will make him feel right at home, as they have previous with prisoners. On a tour to Jamaica recently the east London club played against a prison team in Kingston and, due to the visitors having to fetch all the balls that went out of the ground because of the reluctance of the opposition to do so with trained rifles on them, they lost by 40-odd runs. Apparently it was a rather moody experience, so it could be a good job that the result went against Wanstead.

CHRIS LEWIS

The ex-England all-rounder could have had it all, yet ended up with a thirteen-year sentence for importing liquid cocaine from St Lucia. Having £140,000 worth in his possession went down fairly badly with the judge, hence the hefty sentence. In hindsight, Lewis should have tried to smuggle cannabis in and claimed that he'd become a disciple of Rastafarianism, but unfortunately for the ex-Surrey and Leicestershire player, no religion I know of extols the virtues of snorting 'gak' in the bogs.

LESLIE GEORGE HYLTON

The only cricketer to be hanged, Hylton played 6 Tests between 1935 and 1939 and was later executed for the murder of his wife, Lurlene. No doubt the wives back in 1955 were just as unimpressed with their husbands playing cricket on Saturday and Sunday as they are now. The jury were also unimpressed, this time with his defence that he had been trying to shoot himself but missed, and he went from the gallows humour of a cricket dressing room to the real gallows. Rumours that Mitchell Johnson is planning a similar defence in the future are completely unfounded.

PHiL TUFNELL AND JAMiE SYKES

Jamie Sykes was Tuffers' spin twin in the late 1980s at Middlesex, often getting a game when Edmonds or Emburey were on Test duty. Described as 'the sort of bloke you could call if someone owed you money and wanted things speeded up a little', Sykes was famous for telling Simon Hughes that 'he could play Malcolm Marshall with my cock'. Tuffers and Sykes once did a runner from a car in the East End one night, having had way too much to drink, and spent a night in the cells. Tuffers allegedly got away, but the not-so-sprightly Sykes was collared by a WPC in Whitechapel before her colleague apprehended the not-so-slow, slow left-armer.

TERRY JENNER

Having been given a gigantic headache by John Snow when he was pinned in 1970/71, Warnie's coach, Terry Jenner, found that eighteen years later his love of the gee-gees had got the better of him. Nicking from his employer to fund his habit, he received six years in 1988, but did only eighteen months. Jenner claimed that it saved his life and he became the coach and mentor to one of the finest players to have bowled a cricket ball.

ViCTORiA, 2010

Staying in Australia, when the gangland killer Carl Williams was hacked to death in Victoria in 2010 whilst serving a prison sentence, an internal inquiry discovered that the guards didn't see anything as they were too busy playing indoor cricket. One hand, one bounce and playing with the stump are well known during rain breaks with every club player, but for the prison warders in Australia, taking your guard is a different matter.

THE SCRIBES

The final section concerns the characters of the cricketing press. Over the years there have been many characters, such as E.W. Swanton and John Arlott, and the growth of cricket blogs have spawned many amateur writers who now write professionally on the game. While the reputation of cricketing journalists liking a drink or three may not be as it was a few years back, there are still plenty of prolific writers out there. Some of these are good, some bad.

One thing I have always tried to do at The Middle Stump is to make my work stand out; in essence, make it characteristic. There are many bland cricket writers out there, and often if you read one of their reports, you've read them all. One writer who is a prolific tweeter, whilst writing valid, current, up-to-date and newsworthy stories, would fall into this category and I often give up reading their pieces halfway through.

Whilst I may not be Oxbridge educated (and *Wisden* I most certainly am not), I hope that my writing stands out from the crowd and isn't the bland, safety-first, atypical prose written by many scribes out there. Being a lad from a working-class part of the country seems to have got up the noses of some of the public school-educated cricketing cognoscenti, but I write what I want, mixing the world of sport and comedy – even if I have sailed close to the legal wind a few times. The majority out there seem to enjoy the work, with nearly 10,000 global followers as of July 2014, along with nearly half a million hits on the website.

My favourite writers have to be those from the *Daily Telegraph*, although not Jonathan Liew, who snootily dismissed my book *Cricket Banter* in December 2013. God knows what he will make of this offering! My favourite, bar none, is Steve James, and not just because he played for the Glamorgan so loved by my co-author of *Cricket Banter*, Liam. 'Sid' was an interviewee in that book, and is an outstanding journo, albeit one called a geek by the current Glammy players. Steve jokingly tells me that he prefers writing on rugby as opposed to cricket as it takes less time. His favoured style is that of sarcasm and wit, although the compassion shown when the son of his close friend and ex-teammate Matthew Maynard passed away in June 2012 brought tears to the eye. Choosing his words carefully, James' column in the *Sunday Telegraph* tends to change in style from week to week and is always fresh and readable, although he still looks like Chris de Burgh …

Derek Pringle is another who writes from the sarcastic angle, and is one of the best writers around at present, even if he is not on Graeme Swann's Christmas card list next year. A fan of the Smiths, Pring likes it when I throw a Morrissey line into my own work, and is also one of the more cultured writers out there.

Mike Selvey from the *Guardian* is another of my favourites, and again, was one of the interviewees in *Cricket Banter*. A real ale fan, Selve is knowledgeable about the game and has a memory like an elephant, often quoting obscure players from the 1980s, like Courtney Ricketts, Norman Featherstone, Derek Turner or Alex Barnett. Luckily, his writing gives away far more than the parsimonious seamer's bowling did in One Day finals.

Selvey mentioned to me that he likes the fact that there is an online growth in the cricket-writing world, and journalism has become a global feature. In the old days a report of a Benson & Hedges zonal game between Derbyshire and Northamptonshire, for instance, would have only been read by the most avid supporter of either county via their local press. Now, the likes of 1.3 billion people in the cricketing-mad country of India, as well as many more in the rest of the world can see the result, and this is also one of the reasons why The Middle Stump has prospered. The growth of online cricket journalism will only get bigger.

On the tabloid side, John Etheridge always gets a decent story, and used to play in the same school side as Alec Stewart. Ethers gave me a brilliant interview in March 2014, and regularly looks to define between cricket journalists, bloggers and the likes. I have made it clear on numerous occasions that I am merely a writer, relaying the odd story that I have picked up over the years and definitely in no way a journalist. Journos get stories and find information, while the rest of us are like vultures following the ailing wildebeest, often having to wait until the hyenas from Fleet Street have had their pick at the carcass.

In terms of radio broadcasting, Phil Tufnell stands out and gives an interesting viewpoint, but Aggers is not my cup of tea. I find him out of touch and, in my opinion, happy to bow down to the ECB paymasters who rule whether the Beeb get the gig or not. Many people like Aggers, and I respect their opinion; he's just not for me.

Two of the online chaps well worth a follow are George Dobell and the Australian, Jarrod Kimber, who both write for 'ESPN Cricinfo'. Dobell is one never afraid to show his true colours, especially following a poor England defeat. His column (the written one) is one that I always turn to and he is worth following on Twitter. George will write from a completely different angle to most, and picks up things that many other writers tend to miss. Kimber is more subtle, but a piss-taker at heart with a profound knowledge of the game, and doesn't tend to write from the jingoistic viewpoint that many Aussies undertake (says me here, who is never parochial, biased or patriotic …). Both he and Dobell are the future of journalism in cricket, and their writing makes them stand out.

The people mentioned above are as much characters of cricket and part of the fabric of the game as any who currently take to the pitch, and those in the chapters before them.

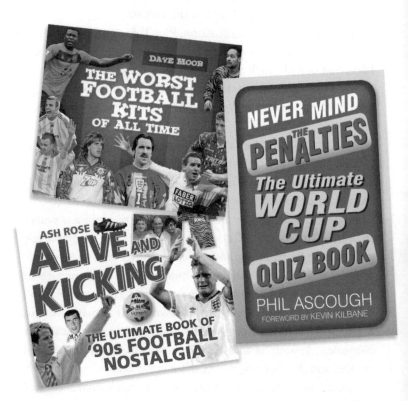